This book is to be returned on or before
the last date stamped below.

3 1 OCT 2011

6613/x

Past-into-Present Series

CHARITIES

Anne Daltrop

B.T. BATSFORD LTD London

First published 1978
© Anne Daltrop 1978

ISBN 0 7134 1040 X

Printed in Great Britain by
The Anchor Press Ltd, Tiptree, Essex
for the Publishers B T Batsford Ltd,
4 Fitzhardinge Street, London W1H 0AH

Acknowledgment

The Author and Publishers would like to thank the following for their kind permission to reproduce copyright illustrations: Age Concern for fig 58; the British Council for fig 51; Community Service Volunteers for figs 61-2; the Mansell Collection for figs 1, 28, 36, 39, 55 (also the frontispiece); Mary Evans Picture Library for figs 6, 8, 10, 11, 13, 16, 25-7, 29, 31-2, 35, 40-1; the National Society for Mentally Handicapped Children for figs 49 (photograph by Mac Campeanu), 63 (photograph by Nick Hedges); the National Trust for fig 18; Oxfam for figs 52, 53 (photograph by Carolyn Watson) and 56 (photograph by Nick Fogden); Popperfoto for fig 66; Radio Times Hulton Picture Library for figs 2-5, 7, 9, 12, 14-15, 17, 19, 21-4, 30, 33-4, 37-8, 42-6; the *Richmond and Twickenham Times* for figs 54, 57, 59, 60 (photograph by Times Photographic Service); the Royal National Life-Boat Institution for fig 50; the Spastics Society for fig 48 (photograph by Maria Bartha); Thomas Coram Foundation for Children for fig 20; Voluntary Service Overseas for figs 64-5; Women's Royal Voluntary Service and *The Western Gazette*, Yeovil, for fig 47 (photograph by L. Britton).

Contents

The Illustrations

Introduction

Look about in any town or village in the British Isles and you will find plenty of evidence of past and present charitable activity. Hospitals, almshouses, schools, public libraries and parks, the familiar landmarks of the areas where we live, were often built or endowed with lands or revenues by philanthropic men or women who intended that many people should benefit from them. In the twentieth century, the state, through central and local government authorities, has assumed responsibility for many of these communal services, and for the welfare of people who through age, sickness or misfortune are unable to care for themselves.

Before the days of the 'Welfare State' however, those in need had to rely entirely upon the goodwill and charitable feelings of their neighbours. In every generation there have been individuals and groups of people who have responded to the need to protect the poor and the destitute.

Gradually, as society became more cohesive and more self-aware, the community as a whole began to accept that it had a responsibility for its less fortunate members, either by voluntary action, or through government intervention. But the extension of the responsibilities of government has been a slow process. Even during the eighteenth and nineteenth centuries, when population increases and the growth of an urban, industrial society made the need desperately urgent, the response was slow and charitable organizations had to bridge the gaps until state services were provided.

Charities pioneered the way in practically every public welfare service we enjoy today, and in the twentieth century voluntary organizations continue to seek out new needs and to extend the limits of community care. This book will look at the successes and the failures of charitable efforts to meet society's needs, faced with wars, epidemics, population increases and economic change.

What makes people give away their fortunes — and their time — in helping others? Benevolence has never been the only motive for charity. As in every sphere of human activity, many motives are present. From early Christian times, for example, charitable gifts have been inspired by strong religious feelings and by the promptings of the church. During the Middle Ages in particular, these religious motives for charity were predominant.

1
Christian Charity in the Middle Ages

In medieval England, looking after the poor was not considered to be the responsibility of the king — that is, the state — and so it was fortunate that the Christian church accepted the task, as part of its concern for the spiritual well-being of mankind. From very early times, church leaders preached that it was the duty of each person to help to care for the poor and the destitute, and that kings and noblemen should set a good example by contributing the largest share.

In Anglo-Saxon England, for example, the king held open house for several days at a time, at Christmas, Easter and Whitsuntide, when food was given to all the needy people who gathered at his gates.

1   An Anglo-Saxon nobleman and his wife hand out food to the poor.

According to the teachings of the church, owning land and property involved responsibilities and was a stewardship from God. To withhold alms from someone in need could be a mortal sin, while poverty itself was not to be despised, since it was the blessed state in which Christ himself had lived. The Royal Maundy service at which the sovereign hands out 'doles' or gifts of red and white purses to old people, is a modern reminder of a much earlier ceremony, in which the king followed Christ's example by distributing loaves and fishes to the poor, and by humbly washing and kissing their feet.

2 Distributing the Royal Maundy in the Palace of Whitehall. The bread and fish were set out on long tables in front of the poor.

Pious and devout people continued to accept their charitable duties throughout the Middle Ages. In the thirteenth century, for example, Eleanor de Montfort, the wealthy wife of Simon, Earl of Leicester, kept detailed household accounts which show that she was very generous in carrying out her charitable obligations. She appointed an almoner to take charge of her gifts to the poor, and in 1265, she gave away an average of four pence a day, as well as food from her table, including thick slices of gravy-soaked bread, called manchets, on which each person placed his helping of meat.

The church also taught that giving to the poor could help to bring forgiveness for sins. Charity could therefore be looked upon as a sound investment. In the words of the ancient Lyke-wake Dirge:

> If ever thou gavest meat or drinke
> every nighte and alle
> The Fire shall never make thee shrinke
> and Christe receive thy saule.

3   King Edward the Confessor blessing a leper.

However, although everyone who was able, was expected to help the poor, their general care and protection was still accepted to be the special duty of the church itself.

The Parish

According to the early Christian fathers, one third of the church's revenue was to be set aside for 'God's poor and needy men in thralldom'. Each parish priest was expected to provide for the poor of his parish, either from the offerings on Sundays, from church lands, or from the 'tithe' which was the ten per cent 'tax' on the produce of each parishioner which went to the church.

Later the parish might provide livestock — a few cattle or sheep — for the repair of the church and the relief of the poor; sometimes a 'church-ale' might be held, a lively gathering at which the ale brewed from corn contributed by the parishioners was sold to raise money for the poor.

By the twelfth century, society had become more peaceful and better organized. The manorial law of land tenure and inheritance offered the peasant and his family some protection; a villein who became too old to work was usually granted the produce of part of the land on which he had worked and a cottage to live in; a widow was entitled to her husband's land without paying the normal inheritance tax to the Lord of the Manor. For cases of real destitution there were the charitable foundations of the church itself.

The Monastery

From the eighth century onwards, monasteries were being founded in Britain and in most of them the relief of the poor was one of the duties laid down in the rules of the order. An almoner was appointed to distribute alms of food or money to those who came to the gates for help. When new clothes or shoes were given to the monks, the almoner handed out the old ones to the poor, together with all the scraps left over from meals. Sometimes the almoner and his helpers visited and fed the sick and the elderly in the villages beyond the monastery gates.

The monastery also offered hospitality to travelling merchants and pilgrims. 'Guests are to be received as if they were Christ Himself' says the Rule of St Benedict. At one time, St Alban's Abbey, on the Great North Road out of London, had stabling for 300 horses and gave all travellers free hospitality for two days. Many of these grateful travellers gave money to the monks for distribution to the poor, often at certain specified times, for example on the anniversary of the donor's death, or they entrusted bequests to the monks for the upkeep of the poor boys, who were taught in the almonry school, or of the poor residents or 'bedesmen' who were lodged in the hospitium.

Hospitals

In the peaceful and fairly prosperous conditions of the twelfth and thirteenth centuries, kings and bishops, wealthy merchants and municipal gilds followed the teaching of the church and founded charitable institutions, or bequeathed land to endow charitable foundations. Many of these foundations were hospitals.

At first the hospital was a building within the gates of a monastery, but gradually it became an independent establishment. Medieval hospitals were places of general hospitality; their services were for the old and needy and for travellers too poor to afford an inn, as well as for the sick. Those intended for the aged and infirm were called almshouses, bedehouses, *Maisons Dieu*, or God's Houses. Some were orphanages, lying-in hospitals for women, or leper colonies.

Two of the most famous of London's present-day hospitals for the sick were founded during the twelfth century. In 1123, Rahere, one of Henry I's courtiers, was taken ill with malarial fever while on a pilgrimage to Rome. He vowed that if he recovered he would found a hospital for the sick and on his safe return home he persuaded the king to grant him a site for his hospital in Smithfield, just outside London. He himself became master of the hospital, which he called St Bartholomew's, while his friend Alfrune collected gifts of money and food; records show that Alfrune persuaded butchers in the near-by market to supply the patients with meat.

St Thomas's Hospital, now housed in modern buildings near to Westminster Bridge, was originally a monastic foundation, staffed by Augustinian monks and nuns. Its site in Southwark was close to London Bridge, the busy main route into the capital from the south and the start of the pilgrim route to Canterbury.

4   A crowded hospital ward, about 1500.

5 Matilda, Henry I's Queen, built a leper hospital and cared for the patients herself.

Many leper hospitals were founded during Norman times, when the disease was widespread. Matilda the 'Good Queen', Henry I's pious wife, was especially concerned with the care of lepers. She built a hospital for them at St Giles-in-the-Fields, London, where she herself washed their feet and kissed their sores. Many leper hospitals were founded and administered by the Order of St Lazarus of Jerusalem and were known as Lazar houses. By the end of the twelfth century, lepers were strictly segregated; a leper had to signal his approach with a clapper or bell and to stand downwind of anyone he spoke to. The victims of leprosy were greatly pitied and many bequests were made to them. For example, Henry II's son William Longspée left a gift of cattle to five leper hospitals in 1226, and nearly two centuries later Bartholomew Neve, a London clothier who died in 1401, left each leper in the Southwark leper house a tunic of russet cloth and twelve pence.

In the early Middle Ages it was usual for the insane to be admitted to the same hospitals as the sick in body. The first separate establishment for them was the Hospital of St Mary of Bethlehem, later known as Bedlam. Many fifteenth-century wills record legacies for 'the poor mad men of Bethlehem'.

Hospitals were largely dependent on these charitable bequests, although some of them received regular contributions from the king, from a patron, or from the rents of lands or houses. A number of hospitals also raised money by holding annual fairs. In 1211, King John authorized the leper hospital of St Mary Magdalene to hold the famous Stourbridge fair near Cambridge. At Carlisle, the hospital was granted the right to a pot of ale from every brew-house and a farthing loaf from each baker. At Shrewsbury market, the lepers were entitled to a handful of corn and flour from every sackful brought for sale. Collecting boxes were hung at hospital gates; one from Harbledown Hospital near Canterbury, where for three-and-a-half centuries pilgrims gave alms to the lepers, has survived until the present day. Sometimes a hospital proctor armed with a special warrant from the bishop or king, would travel the countryside, collecting on behalf of a particular hospital.

Educating the Poor

The church also cared for and educated poor orphans. The first schools were in monasteries, or were song schools attached to abbeys or cathedrals. Parish priests or chantry priests often taught the neighbourhood children. Chantries were a popular way of obtaining prayers for the soul of the founder and his family during the fourteenth and fifteenth centuries. The chantry was maintained by a bequest or a gift of land and the chantry priest was usually expected to give away alms and to teach the children of the poor as well. By the time of the Reformation in the sixteenth century, there were 2,000 chantry schools in England and Wales.

Other schools and colleges were endowed too. In 1270 Walter Merton, the Chancellor of England, built and endowed Merton College, Oxford, as a home

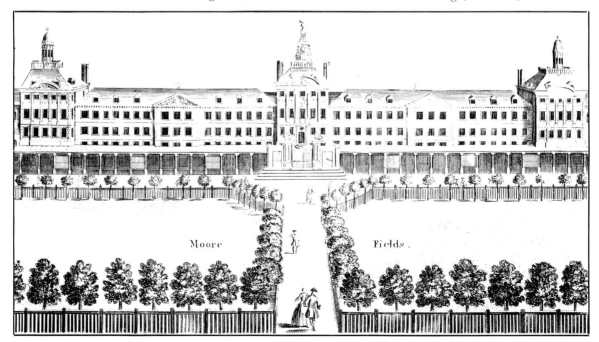

for 30 students of theology, and as an act of penance, John de Balliol, a wealthy baron, who died in 1263, and his wife Devaguila, a Scottish princess, also left lands for the endowment of a college at Oxford.

The Town and the Gild

Since Anglo-Saxon times, there were semi-religious gilds or fraternities in most parishes, which helped their members in misfortune, with 'burial benefit', for example, or for a specific purpose, like the Pilgrim Gilds, which enabled their members to go on pilgrimages. Later, merchant and craft gilds helped their members to get started in trade, or in sickness or unemployment. They also built almshouses, which soon succeeded hospitals as the most popular charitable foundations.

Medieval York had the largest number of almshouses outside London. Most were supported by local gilds like the Merchant Venturers or the Mercers. St Leonard's Hospital in York became the largest almshouse in England, providing a home for over 200 bedesmen, 30 choristers and two school teachers, as well as for the 13 monks and nuns who ran it.

By the fourteenth century, most boroughs had their own almshouses for the aged poor. Local records in Rye and Winchelsea in Sussex, for example, show that men and women 'of good repute and no goods or chattels' were received without payment into the towns' hospitals.

Prosperous merchants were often outstandingly generous towards their fellow citizens. Perhaps the most famous was Richard Whittington who was three times Lord Mayor of London in the fifteenth century. When he died in 1423, he created a trust for the old and the poor, which lasted for 500 years.

6 *Left* Bethlem Hospital, which was originally founded in 1246, was granted to the citizens of London by Henry VIII as a hospital for the insane.

7 Merton College, Oxford, was built and endowed by Walter Merton, the Chancellor of England, 1270.

He appointed his own gild, the Mercers, as trustees, while his great friend and executor, John Carpenter, was kept busy carrying out other bequests. Carpenter used Whittington's money and some of his own too, to found a library at the Guildhall, to build an almshouse and a college for priests, and to repair part of the prison at Newgate.

Road and Bridge Charities

Responsibility for the care of roads rested with the lord of the manor, or with the township through which they passed. When the local lord was neglectful, the road soon turned into a quagmire and often the nearest monastery would maintain the road, since the monks needed to be able to travel easily between their various estates.

Bridges too were necessary for the clergy and for pilgrims on their travels. Sometimes a local priest, or a recluse like the hermit at Beccles in Suffolk, would build a stone bridge to replace an earlier wooden one, or religious gilds of laymen, like the Gild of the Holy Cross at Birmingham, would make themselves responsible for bridge and road repairs. Since early times, the Church had offered indulgences — relief from the performance of certain religious duties — in return for this help with the upkeep of roads and bridges. Many fifteenth-century wills survive which record gifts left for road and bridge maintenance. John Blot, a citizen of London, left £5 'to be yspendyth between London and Ware, of fowle ways. . . there most nede is'. In Nottingham, the sheriff appointed two bridge-wardens to care for the ancient Hesketh Bridge, and to administer the funds given to it. In the little chapel on the bridge a priest would celebrate a daily mass on behalf of all helpers and benefactors of the bridge. Even after the Reformation, gifts for mending highways and bridges continued. At Kingston in Surrey, many bequests were left to maintain the great bridges and the highway over the River Thames.

The Range of Medieval Charity

William Langland, the fourteenth-century poet, demonstrated the wide range of medieval charity in his advice to rich merchants, worried about the fate of their eternal souls:

> . . . repair hospitals,
> help sick people,
> mend bad roads
> build up bridges that had been broken down,
> help maides to marry or to make them nuns,
> find food for prisoners and poor people,
> put scholars to school or to some other craft,
> help religious orders, and
> ameliorate rents and taxes. . .

Perhaps the most popular charity of all was the gift or 'dole', for distribution on the anniversary of death, or at the funeral, of the donor. The dole might be for a thousand loaves of bread, or a penny each to a hundred men, in return for a prayer for the soul of the benefactor.

Alms were often handed out on a huge scale. One bishop of Ely gave away bread, drink and warm meat to 200 people each day. When doles were distributed after the funerals of notable people, the crowds were often so large and unruly that accidents happened. In 1322, 55 people were crushed to death when they scrambled for their share of the doles given for the soul of Henry Fingue, a former fishmonger and sheriff of London.

The Decline of Medieval Charity

These charities were haphazard and were often criticized as being demoralizing for the poor. By the fourteenth century there was growing criticism of the monasteries too, which were isolated centres of charity and not numerous enough to deal with poverty as a whole. It was felt that those who received charity were not investigated carefully enough. Vagabonds were said to be 'travelling from spital to spital, prowling and poaching for lumps of bread and meat'. There were complaints that crowds of miserable, idle or crippled people, covered with rags and filth, were collecting around the gates of the great monastic foundations.

The church in the fourteenth century was led by worldly bishops and popes and its standards began to decline. Kings and patrons used their influence to give to their own servants places in hospitals and almshouses which should have gone to the old and sick. Medieval bequests were forgotten or misused. Religious zeal and public generosity both declined and hospitals and alms-houses began to close down.

At the same time, the manorial system of land tenure was falling into disuse, depriving the old and sick of the security it had given them. More craftsmen began to work for wages and were subject to unemployment when trade was bad. A series of epidemics in Western Europe, the most serious of which was the Black Death, which decimated the population of England in the years 1348-9, caused labour shortages and a rise in wages. Parliament passed laws to try to force the able-bodied to work and to keep wages at their old levels. At the same time, they tried to control begging by forbidding the giving of alms to able-bodied beggars, who were to be punished. 'Impotent' or disabled beggars were to be sent back to and supported by the parish where they were born.

From the middle of the fifteenth century, English society lacked sufficient resources to deal with poverty, at a time when a new kind of pauper, the vagrant without home, skill or employment, was causing general concern.

2
Benevolent Merchants and Country Gentlemen

The Problem of Vagrancy

Between 1520 and 1640, vagrancy and the difficulties of the homeless poor became the most pressing social problem in England. A survey carried out in 1517 showed that there were over 1,000 beggars in London alone. Many towns tried to control begging. The helpless or 'impotent' poor were issued with badges and licences to beg. Hundreds of licences were granted by the

8   In the sixteenth and seventeenth centuries, the growing number of vagrants and beggars became a serious social problem.

London Court of Aldermen. In Southampton, licensed beggars were provided with a livery, or uniform, and a head beggar was appointed to supervise the badged beggars and to punish 'valiant or sturdy rogues'. But it was clear that the problem was still growing. The population was increasing rapidly and vagrancy was becoming a serious threat to law and order. Parliament and the King's Privy Council were forced to intervene.

In 1536, Parliament ordered all local justices to issue begging licences, to punish all able-bodied beggars who were then to be returned to the parish where they were born, and to prohibit the giving of doles. Voluntary contributions for supporting the deserving poor were to be collected in churches on Sundays.

Charities and the Reformation

The medieval church had taught that alms for the poor were better distributed through the church. But by the time of Henry VIII's quarrel with the Pope in 1527, many people were already deeply concerned over the decline of ecclesiastical standards and with the mismanagement of some of the charitable institutions under church control.

9 Able-bodied beggars, or 'Sturdy Rogues', were punished and sent back to the parishes where they were born.

After Henry VIII's break with the papacy therefore, responsibility for the care of the poor was transferred from the religious houses to the crown. As part of the process of 'breaking the bonds with Rome', Parliament agreed to the suppression of the monasteries, by Acts of Parliament passed between 1536 and 1539, and in 1545, to the passing of an Act which dissolved the chantries, free chapels, hospitals and gilds. Monasteries, hospitals and chantries which had formerly belonged to the church were granted to the king and his heirs, and Parliament was confident that those who had been looked after in them would be better off under royal benevolence.

The immediate effect of the dissolution of the monasteries, however, was to create yet more vagrants, for although monks and priests were pensioned off, the tenants and servants of the church foundations became destitute, at a time when inflation was causing prices to outstrip wages and the population was rising rapidly.

In the long run, the reformation stimulated charity into new life by bringing medieval institutions under secular control. For the Tudor monarchs passed on their new responsibilities to the community and it was the merchants and country gentlemen of Tudor and Stuart England who were expected to shoulder the main burden of care for the poor.

Reformation preachers, especially the London bishops, Latimer and Ridley, taught that it was the responsibility of each individual to care for his fellows who were in need. Within a generation of the dissolution of the monasteries, contributions to charity had been more than made up by private benefactors, whose motives were often still religious, although they now generally gave to non-religious charities. Sixteenth-century merchants and gentry were very conscientious in accepting their social responsibilities. By the end of the century, the prosperous Englishman was expected to leave a substantial proportion of his wealth to charity and failure to do so was regarded as remiss. From 1540 onwards, tracts and sermons preached by both Anglicans and Puritans put great emphasis on the Christian duty of charity, 'a doctrine obvious to all' in John Donne's words. Christians who ignored it were guilty of oppressing the weak and the poor.

In London, 24 citizens presented King Henry VIII with a report on pauperism in the city and the king was persuaded to give the 'Royal' Hospitals of St Bartholomew, St Thomas, and Bethlehem to the city for the care of the sick poor, and the former royal palace of Bridewell as a house of correction for the 'idle and vicious'. Although the hospitals were partly endowed by the king, the citizens had to support them too. St Bartholomew's was re-endowed by the Common Council of London with 500 marks annually and the citizens of London agreed to raise a similar sum each year. Later the hospital was granted an annual amount from the profits of the City's cloth market at Blackwell Hall and all the profits of the beams, or weighing machines, used by merchants who brought goods into the city.

Bishop Nicholas Ridley, who had great influence over Edward VI, the young son of Henry VIII, insisted on the need for adequate provision for London's orphans. He helped to found Christ's Hospital, for 'fatherless orphans and poor mens children'. Edward VI gave it a home, the former convent of Greyfriars, and a royal charter giving it the right to hold property in perpetuity, but the running costs had to be raised by the citizens, through weekly church collections and the levying of taxes. A scrutineer was appointed to persuade people to leave legacies to it and Christ's Hospital has survived into the twentieth century, as a great public school which still helps to educate orphaned children.

Tudor monarchs encouraged these charitable activities as a safeguard against possible disturbances of the peace. Although pity and care for the poor were important, they were far more worried about the threat which poverty and vagrancy offered to the maintenance of law and order. In the reign of Elizabeth, when there was a long period of peace and freedom from outbreaks of plague, much thought was given to the causes of poverty, which culminated in a great debate in Parliament in 1597 on the state of the nation. It led to the framing of an Elizabethan Poor Law, which was to remain the basis of English poor law administration until the nineteenth century. It was based on the parish, where the local justices of the peace were expected to put the law into effect. Two overseers of the poor were appointed in each parish to collect the poor rate from each household and to distribute it to those in need. The voluntary contributions introduced earlier in the century became a compulsory poor rate, which was to be levied in times of national emergency. So there was now a system of compulsory contributions to help the poor in times of crisis, but at other times charity was still considered adequate for relieving suffering, educating the young and dealing with all other social problems. The Elizabethan Poor Laws of 1601 were accompanied by a statute designed to protect charitable gifts and bequests from misuse.

The Statute of Charitable Uses
Ever since the thirteenth century, gifts and bequests for religious purposes had been placed under the trusteeship of the religious orders and the ecclesiastical courts were responsible for their administration. Gradually the idea of

10 King Edward VI presenting the charter to Christ's Hospital.

trusteeship was applied to secular as well as religious purposes. A testator might entrust property to another person, to be used for purposes held by the law to be charitable. If the court agreed that the objects of a trust were charitable, gifts to it could be accepted in perpetuity, that is, they could exist for ever, whereas other bequests were strictly limited in time.

Early in the fifteenth century, the Court of Chancery, under its president, the Lord Chancellor, had taken over responsibility for charitable bequests from the church's own courts. It represented the king, who as 'parens patria' had taken charitable gifts and the interests of 'infants and lunatics' under his special care. By this time, the mass of bequests of money, land and property left to charities since the early Middle Ages was causing the lawyers a great deal of work.

The Elizabethan Statute of Charitable Uses of 1601 codified the laws relating to charity. It listed a wide variety of purposes that were to be considered charitable and offered them favourable treatment. Special commissioners were appointed to look into and correct possible abuses. The courts worked on the assumption that the aim of the donor was to 'benefit his own soul by charitable works'. If the original purpose of a trust should fail, the courts could specify a new one, as near as possible, *cy près*, in the Norman French of the law courts, the original intention of the donor.

The Elizabethan procedures were used throughout the seventeenth century, and then gradually fell into disuse. But the Preamble to the Act, which listed purposes that could be regarded as charitable, remains the last word in defining a charity legally and is still referred to by the courts although the statute itself has been repealed. These purposes were listed as follows:

> For the relief of aged, impotent and poor people, some for the maintenance of sick and maimed soldiers and mariners, schools of learning, free schools and scholars in universities, some for repair of bridges, ports, havens, causeways, churches, sea-banks and highways, some for education and preferment of orphans, some for or towards relief, stock or maintenance for houses of correction, some for marriages of poor maids, some for supportation, aid and help of young tradesmen, handicraftsmen and persons decayed; and others for relief or redemption of prisoners and captives, and for aid or ease of any poor inhabitant concerning payment of fifteens, setting out of soldiers and other taxes.

Grammar Schools and Scholarships

Instead of supporting monasteries, founding chantries or contributing towards the cost of building a parish church, as their ancestors had done, many Elizabethans contributed towards educational charities. Eighteen grammar schools had already been founded in the reign of Edward VI, with funds raised from the sale of monastic lands. During the reign of Elizabeth, one third of all benevolent gifts were for educational purposes.

Often a school and an almshouse would form part of the same bequest. Charterhouse, for example, founded by Thomas Sutton in a former Carthusian monastery, provided education and maintenance for 40 scholars and 'gown boys' and for 80 old men pensioners. Edward Alleyn, the Elizabethan actor who owned a theatre and a bear-baiting pit in London, bought the manor of Dulwich in 1605. Here he built a chapel, 12 almshouses and a school house, to be called the 'College of God's Gift', for 12 poor scholars, and endowed it with property at Lambeth and Bishopsgate and with an income from his Fortune Theatre.

Many schools were endowed by the townspeople themselves, for example, Shrewsbury School, and the former chantry schools, like that at Penrith, which were refounded under Edward VI and Elizabeth I as town grammar schools. Although the monarch usually gave his name and a charter to the school, the town had to find the money to run it.

Merchants and lawyers founded scholarships and exhibitions for poor boys to study at Oxford. Sir Thomas White, master of the Merchant Taylors Company, who made a fortune through the opening up of trade with Russia and Eastern Europe, established the college of St John's with the proceeds. Henry Hastings, Earl of Huntingdon, a Puritan who was criticized during his lifetime because he 'much wasted his estates by charities', was nevertheless praised in a popular ballad, as follows:

> He built up no palace nor purchased no towne,
>   But gave it to scholars to get him renowne,
> As Oxford and Cambridge can rightly declare,
> How many poor scholars maintained are there.

11 The Charterhouse, formerly a Carthusian monastery, was made into a hospital and school by Sir Thomas Sutton, whose wealth came from the coal mines of Durham.

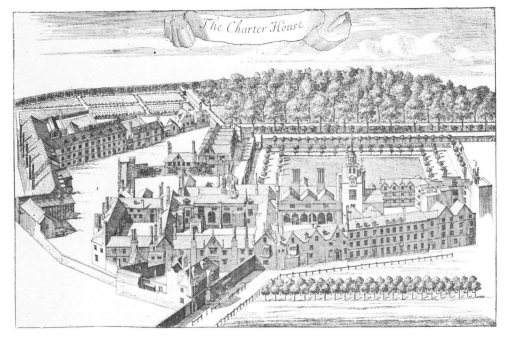

Seventeenth-Century Charities

In the early Stuart period, the ideas and the policies of Elizabeth's reign, resulted in a great outpouring of private charity. Most people still left their money to schools, apprenticeships or almshouses. Among the latter was the Islington foundation of Dame Alice Owen. As a small girl playing in the fields near her home, Alice Owen was nearly killed by an arrow which 'pierced quite throw the hat on her head'. In gratitude for her escape, she later built ten almshouses, a school and a chapel on the very spot where she had been playing years before. Three arrows were fixed to one gable of the building. The Brewers Company were made trustees of lands in Islington and Clerkenwell to provide for the upkeep of the foundation.

Charities for the distribution of Bibles to young people or for copies to be chained in church pews, show how the new translations of the Bible were reaching people throughout the country. Lectures and sermons were popular, often reflecting the growing influence of puritanism in England. The usual amount for a bequest for a sermon was 6s 8d, but a certain Joan Smales of Shoreditch left 10s for the preacher and 20s to be distributed among those who came to listen to him!

Many early seventeenth-century merchants were influenced by Puritan teaching on the worth of individual action and enterprise. Work, service to the community, order and discipline in society, were all part of this Puritan attitude to life. Their piety and generosity was praised by John Stow in his *Survey of London* and by Thomas Fuller whose *History of the Worthies of England* described the great charitable benefactions and the men who made them.

Nicholas Ferrar's charity was religiously inspired. He was a business man and member of Parliament who grew tired of the bitterness of public life and moved with his family to the manor of Little Gidding in Huntingdonshire.

12 *Left* Many merchants like Sir Thomas White, founder of St John's College, Oxford, endowed schools and colleges in the sixteenth and seventeenth centuries.

13 *Below* Trinity Almshouses in the East End of London. Many similar almshouses were founded by private benefactors in the seventeenth century.

In 1626, he was ordained in the Anglican church and founded a religious community at Little Gidding. Here the family ran a dispensary and an infirmary where medicines and treatment were given free of charge to the local people. The Ferrar daughters organized a Sunday morning school, where the children were given a penny and their Sunday dinner, if they remembered a psalm by heart. The community kept itself by bookbinding for twenty years, until it was broken up by parliamentary troops in 1647.

After the Civil War, there were many new ideas about society and property, but most charitable endowments during the Commonwealth continued to be for schools, almshouses and apprenticeships. Most were still inspired by religious motives, though few now gave to the church itself or to its ministers. Godly men gave their wealth to the poor, to beautify their cities and to endow the educational system.

14 The Society of Friends or 'Quakers' was founded during the Commonwealth. Its members have since been closely associated with many of the great philanthropic movements, including the struggle against slavery, for penal reform and for universal education.

George Fox, who founded the Society of Friends (the Quakers) during the Commonwealth, insisted on the need for service to the underprivileged. In his journal written in 1660, he describes how efforts were made to attract the poor to Quaker meetings, and to give them food after the meetings.

The Plague and the Fire of London

The plague outbreak of 1665 disrupted trade and caused unemployment among the survivors. Thomas Firmin, a London mercer, mistrusted alms-giving, and believed in providing work and a means of livelihood to reduce social distress. He founded a workshop for the unemployed, provided raw linen for spinning and weaving and sold the finished cloth at cost price. At one time his workshops employed over 1,700 spinners and weavers. Later in the 1680s he started a similar workshop for refugee French Huguenots in Ipswich.

The Great Fire of London in 1666, aroused sympathy and offers of help for Londoners from all over the country. A Lancashire apprentice named Roger Lowe, for example, canvassed his village and made a list of the people who were willing to help those in need. Gifts of money poured into London, and 'to the amazement of all Europe', the City of London was rebuilt within four years of the fire.

Sometimes 'Charity Briefs' were issued on behalf of the needy. These were a common method of fund raising in Tudor and Stuart times. Sufferers from fire, flood or plague could apply to the king or to Parliament for the issue of a Royal Warrant, authorizing a special collection, usually in church on Sunday mornings. Charity Briefs were widely used until the establishment of fire insurance offices towards the end of the seventeenth century.

15 After the Great Fire of London in 1666 money was collected from all over England to help with the rebuilding.

3
Joint Action in the Eighteenth Century

Charitable Societies

England grew prosperous in the last years of the seventeenth century. Her overseas trade developed rapidly and her agriculture was productive. Business men discovered the uses of the joint stock company and the excitement of investment. Because the economy was expanding, it seemed to many people that, since there was work for all, only the idle needed to be out of work and therefore there was a growing impatience with the poor. In 1704, Daniel Defoe wrote a pamphlet called *Giving Alms no Charity* which won him much popularity; in it he declared that idleness was the most common cause of poverty and was only encouraged by almsgiving.

The eighteenth century was an age of religious compromise, in sharp contrast to the deep differences of the sixteenth and seventeenth centuries. More easy-going attitudes led to religious toleration, but they also led to complacency and to indifference towards suffering, and to a widespread lack of charitable concern. The poor were seen by many as a burden, rather than as subjects for care.

However, charitable people exist in every age, and in the early eighteenth century they began to experiment with new ways of raising funds for charity. In the sixteenth and seventeenth centuries, individual Englishmen had given wealth to charity in the form of the charitable trust. In the eighteenth century, they began to apply the new methods used in business to charities. Charitable societies and associations were formed which opened subscription lists similar to the lists of shareholders in commercial companies and individual donors were invited to contribute. People were delighted to discover that their small subscriptions of a guinea or two could accumulate to show very solid results, and contributions to charitable societies, rather than individual endowments, became the most common form of giving to charity.

Charity Schools and Sunday Schools

The new fund-raising methods were first applied to charity schools. In 1698, the Anglican Society for Promoting Christian Knowledge (SPCK) was founded by the Rev. Thomas Bray and his friends to teach children the Protestant religion and 'the habits of industry'. Local representatives of the SPCK opened subscription lists and organized church collections to found and maintain the schools, which were intended to train boys for apprenticeship and girls to be domestic servants. Religious instruction, the three 'rs' and, for girls, sewing and knitting were taught. The schools were most successful in urban areas, particularly in London, where there was a large middle class to support them and work for the children when they left.

A special annual ceremony was held in London to raise extra funds for the schools. Each year from 1707 until the 1870s thousands of charity school-children marched through the streets in their uniforms to a service and collection on their behalf in a city church. The occasion soon became one of the sights of London. Wooden galleries had to be built in St Paul's Cathedral to accommodate the children and the fashionable crowds who packed the church to see their neat and well-behaved protégés. The children also appeared on days of national celebration, for example at the thanksgiving ceremonies to mark the ending of the war against France in 1713, and in honour of the accession of George I to the throne in 1714, when 4,000 charity schoolchildren sat on benches in the Strand and sang hymns.

Child labour was in great demand in the eighteenth century and parents and employers sometimes grudged the time spent in school when children could have been working. Other criticisms were heard. When Hannah More opened a school for miners' children in the Mendips, there was some disapproval because 'the poor were intended to be servants and slaves: it was pre-ordained that they should be ignorant'. Mrs More was able to reassure her critics: 'My plan for instructing the poor is very limited and strict. They learn of weekdays such coarse works as may fit them for servants. I allow no writing'. Mrs Sarah Trimmer, who wrote *The Oeconomy of Charity* to interest ladies in charitable works, considered that educating the labouring classes helped to make them 'useful members of the state, for their services are essential in the greatest degree, to the comfort and convenience of the higher orders of society'.

16 *Left* Charity school-children and their teachers set out for the annual service in St Paul's Cathedral.

17 *Opposite* On entering London in September 1714, George I declared that 'the charity children were one of the finest sights he ever saw in his life'.

By the mid-eighteenth century, there were about 25,000 charity schools throughout the country. In Caxton Street, Westminster the figure of a boy wearing charity school uniform still stands above the doorway of a house where the Westminster Bluecoat School was founded by voluntary contributions in 1688. Nearby, in Greycoat Place, a similar school was founded by local tradesmen.

Towards the end of the century, when the charity school movement had become less active, and many young children were working long hours in factories, Robert Raikes, a newspaper editor in Gloucestershire, founded a Sunday morning school for young textile workers. 'My intention is to make idle, profligate and filthy boys more orderly, tractable and attentive to business' he declared. His ideas were soon copied and other similar schools were founded. Raikes was received by Queen Charlotte and Sunday School Committees were set up all over England; a Sunday School Union was founded in 1803.

The Voluntary Hospitals

The great voluntary hospital movement in Britain also began in the eighteenth century and money to support it was again raised mainly by voluntary subscriptions.

During the seventeenth century, cities, especially London, had grown rapidly. Food shortages, overcrowding and serious epidemics had resulted. Fortunately there were some advances in medical science at the same time.

In 1716, Henry Hoare, a merchant banker, and a number of friends, met in St Dunstan's coffee house in Westminster to discuss ways in which they could help the sick poor. They drew up an appeal for subscriptions and in 1719 were able to set up an infirmary in Petty France, Westminster. Between 1719 and 1746, four more hospitals were built in London, three of them supported by voluntary subscriptions: St George's Hospital, the Middlesex Hospital for smallpox, and the London Hospital in Whitechapel in the East End. Guy's Hospital was the only one of the four to be founded by a single philanthropist. Thomas Guy was a London publisher and bookseller, a bachelor who invested his money and made a great deal out of South Sea Stock before the famous crash. In 1720, he sold £54,000 worth of stock for over £230,000 and used the money to build a hospital for the poor. Thomas Guy made his own rules for his hospital, and any patient found gambling or smoking was immediately discharged.

18 Statue of a Bluecoat Schoolboy. The uniform of long blue gown and yellow stockings was the everyday dress of schoolboys in the first half of the sixteenth century.

The voluntary subscription method of raising money was also used to found hospitals in the provinces. A subscription list was opened in Winchester by a royal donation of £20, and Bristol, York and Exeter soon established their own voluntary hospitals. During the 1770s and 1780s, dispensaries were founded to give free medical advice and treatment to the neighbourhood poor — giving doctors an opportunity to learn a great deal more about the diseases associated with dirt and poverty.

Once established, the hospitals relied for support on legacies, gifts and annual subscriptions. A subscription of five guineas or a lump sum of £30 gave the donor a place on the governing board, the right to vote at board meetings, and the privilege of recommending patients.

Many people contributed guineas and a few dedicated people on each committee, board of governors, or subscription list took a constant interest in the organization and worked very hard to raise further funds, sometimes retiring from business to give more of their time to charitable activities. They organized hospital concerts, which were held in Westminster Abbey and other churches. They persuaded famous actors to give charity performances; David Garrick gave some notable performances of Shakespeare's *Much Ado About Nothing* in aid of the Middlesex Hospital in the 1750s. A sermon was preached annually on behalf of the London Hospital in a city church, followed by a procession to a tavern for a festival dinner, costing 25 guineas a head; in one year in the nineteenth century £26,000 was raised in this way!

The Foundling Child

Thomas Coram was a retired sea captain who went to live in Rotherhithe on the River Thames. On journeys to and from London he would see the bodies of newly-born babies left abandoned on the roadside by unmarried mothers who could not afford to look after their children. Sometimes these foundlings were left in other places about the city. The Inner Temple, where many lawyers lived and worked, eventually had to employ a nurse to look after the babies found abandoned there, many of whom were given the surname 'Temple'.

Thomas Coram decided to spend the rest of his life, if necessary, in establishing a special hospital for foundlings. For 17 years he fought hard for his scheme against the opposition of those who thought that it would lead to more illegitimate births. Eventually he won the support of a group of influential society ladies, and with their help he obtained a royal charter. Coram and his friends made a public appeal for subscriptions and were able to buy several acres of land in Bloomsbury known as 'Coram's Fields' where the new buildings of the Foundling Hospital were opened in 1754.

At first, the children were admitted on a first-come-first-served principle, but soon there were too many of them. Mothers then had to draw a coloured ball out of a hat; those who drew a white ball were the lucky ones. For a short time the hospital received government support, provided that it admitted all the children who were brought. A basket was hung at the gate in Guildford

Street, but on the first day of open admissions 117 children were left nearby. Carriers brought small babies from as far away as Yorkshire. Soon there were 4,000 children in the hospital and many died of infectious diseases, and so the hospital had to go back to its independent status.

The hospital and its grounds became a fashionable meeting place for London society. Excellent sermons were preached in the chapel and Sunday morning services were always well attended. Famous artists like William Hogarth, a close friend of Thomas Coram, Sir Joshua Reynolds and Thomas Gainsborough supported the hospital and donated pictures to it. Handel presented it with an organ for the chapel and frequently played there. He conducted performances of the Messiah in aid of the hospital and left a copy of the score to it when he died.

Coram himself was an outspoken old man who quarrelled with some of the governors and was eventually excluded from the board, but he continued to visit the children to hand round gingerbread. Today the foundation runs a day nursery, a child-care centre and supervised foster homes, and in Coram's Fields there are still playing fields for young people.

Jonas Hanway, who was one of the governors of the Foundling Hospital, also gave all his time to philanthropy when he retired. He persuaded a group of shipowners and merchants to found the Marine Society to apprentice penniless young men and equip them to go to sea. In 1786 the society bought its own training ship. By the beginning of the nineteenth century over 25,000 boys had been trained to serve at sea. Hanway also campaigned on behalf of chimney sweeps' climbing boys, and of the street boys whom he called the 'blackguards', but little was done for them until after his death.

Thomas Coram and Jonas Hanway, like many of their contemporaries, cared little for formal religion. Their benevolence was inspired by generosity and humanitarian views, coupled with the currently popular 'mercantilist' view that England needed a flourishing and healthy population in order to remain prosperous.

19 *Left* Mothers bringing their babies to the Foundling Hospital.

20 Captain Coram, founder of the Foundling Hospital. A portrait by William Hogarth.

Malicious Charity

In every century, charities have been founded for perverse reasons. 'Pride and vanity have built more hospitals than all the virtues together', wrote an eighteenth-century commentator called Bernard Mandeville, and the age in which he lived was particularly rich in examples. They were to cause lawyers and charity administrators endless problems in later years.

Christopher Tancred was a wealthy Yorkshire squire who fell out with his five sisters. In order to prevent his sisters from inheriting his money, he founded Tancred's Hospital, an almshouse for 'decayed gentlemen'. However the charity was badly mismanaged. The buildings were neglected and the old gentlemen were dissatisfied and quarrelled and complained continuously. Throughout the first half of the nineteenth century there were many attempts to suppress the charity, but the law of charities as it then stood would not allow the original intentions of the founder to be overthrown.

George Jarvis, who died in 1793, was outraged by his daughter's marriage and disinherited her and her descendants, and left his £100,000 to the poor of three parishes in Herefordshire. The total population of these villages was under 900, but hundreds of beggars crowded in to share in the regular handouts of money, turning the villages into 'rural slums', according to the angry local residents.

Rousing Popular Opinion

Towards the end of the eighteenth century there was more general concern for suffering and injustice, which showed itself in public campaigns to help prisoners and slaves.

John Howard's book on *The State of the Prisons* described the terrible filth and overcrowding in which most prisoners were forced to live. Prison charities were shown to be quite inadequate to improve such conditions and

21 *Left* William Wilberforce, leader of the campaigns to end the slave trade and slavery, gave away at least one quarter of his income to charity each year.

22 A soup kitchen in Leicester Square, London.

Howard's book led to government intervention to ensure better food and cleanliness and less brutality within the prisons.

Slavery had been accepted during the eighteenth century as a means of increasing trade and producing cheaper sugar, but in 1769, Granville Sharp's book describing his life as a slave led to the formation of a London committee to campaign for abolition of the slave trade, with William Wilberforce as its leader in Parliament. The Anti-Slavery campaign was one of the first attempts to combine charitable objectives with putting pressure on Parliament to achieve social change. Associated with the campaign was a charity called the Sierra Leone Company, founded to colonize that country with ex-slaves and, in 1799, a school for negro boys and girls from Sierra Leone was founded in Clapham to educate the children for posts of responsibility in the colony.

After the French Revolution

Generally speaking however, the conditions of the poor were worse at the end of the eighteenth century than they had been at the beginning. Population increases and land enclosures were adding to unemployment in the countryside. The wars against revolutionary France disrupted trade and pushed up the price of corn.

The French Revolution had alarmed the government and the upper classes. They were aware of the need to relieve poverty in order to prevent the spread of popular violence to Britain. Soup kitchens were set up during the near-famine years of the wars. In Spitalfields, where the silk weavers were suffering great hardships as a result of a war-time trade depression, a Soup Society was founded by the Quakers, who gave out tickets for bread, coal, soup and medical supplies. City companies, banks and office workers contributed generously to them. Some soup societies continued after the war, but criticism was soon heard; the Spitalfield charities were attacked for giving indiscriminately and acting as a magnet for paupers. Malthus, in his *Essay on Population*, had warned his readers that indiscriminate charity only increased the sum of poverty and misery and was against the laws of nature. Few people realized that widespread poverty was the result of profound changes in the society in which they were living.

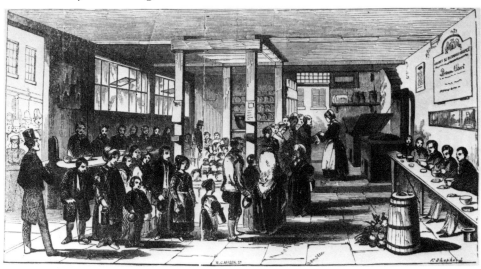

4
Charity in an Urban Industrial Society

Between the 1770s and the 1850s, life for many people in Britain was transformed by the social, economic, industrial and political changes which we call the 'industrial revolution'. Developments in technology and business organization, the expansion of markets at home and abroad, an unprecedented population increase and the growth of big industrial towns all meant that the Victorians were going to need to find answers to a whole series of new social problems.

Thousands of people flocked into London, Birmingham, Liverpool and Manchester from the surrounding countryside to work in factories and workshops. The owners of the new factories needed to recoup the money they had spent on machinery and new buildings. Many did not think of their workers as individuals, but looked upon them as the 'hands', who needed firm control and minimum wages if any profit was to be made. Child labour usually turned out to be the cheapest and easiest to discipline.

Most people did not understand the nature of the changed conditions of their society and the new type of urban poverty they had bred. They still thought of poverty in terms of the agricultural society of southern England, in which the burden of the parish poor rate fell heavily upon the local landowners and farmers. Even in the countryside, the traditional poor law system, which had hardly changed since the reign of Elizabeth, was no longer working. Bread had become so expensive that agricultural workers were not earning enough to live on and large numbers of families had to be supported by poor relief. It was obvious that a new poor law system would have to be devised.

Unfortunately, the commissioners who framed the New Poor Law, in 1834, assumed as their eighteenth-century predecessors had done, that on the whole, poverty was the result of 'fraud, indolence and idleness'. They introduced a harsh new system based on the principle that life inside the parish workhouse must be made more disagreeable than the life of anyone earning a living outside. Only 'paupers' were to be admitted, those who had parted with all their possessions and were completely destitute, and no help was to be given outside the workhouse.

In the countryside this system was harsh and often inappropriate, for most of the applicants were suffering genuine hardship as a result of old age, illness or widowhood — not idleness. In the towns the system did not work at all. Factory workers in northern mill towns, for example, only applied for poor relief occasionally, when a mill was shut down, or when short-time working was introduced. Then hundreds of workers were on relief at the same time, and the workhouse could not possibly accommodate them.

The Victorians had carried over into their urban industrial society the moral attitudes of the eighteenth century. They believed that the working classes must be taught thrift, industry, temperance and family responsibility. Therefore the barest minimum of relief was to be supplied by the authorities. The rest was left to self-help and mutual aid; and where that failed, to charity. During the first half of the nineteenth century, working men who could afford it put aside a portion of their weekly wage in a Friendly Society, for use in emergencies. Later in the century trade unions offered the same facilities. But most factory workers were too irregularly employed or too ill-paid to afford these small weekly contributions.

Charity was still expected to carry the main burden of the welfare of the poor. To many people private charity offered one great advantage over public assistance; it could be stopped at any time and was therefore thought less likely to be misused, or to create bad habits of idleness. Between 1820 and 1860, private charitable organizations tried to cope with the problems of the new urban industrialized society.

Visiting Societies

As prosperity from industry increased among the factory owners and entrepreneurs, middle-class families moved out of the centre of the towns into the suburbs. They avoided the slum areas of cities where the workers lived and where dirt and overcrowding led to outbreaks of typhus and cholera. Gradually

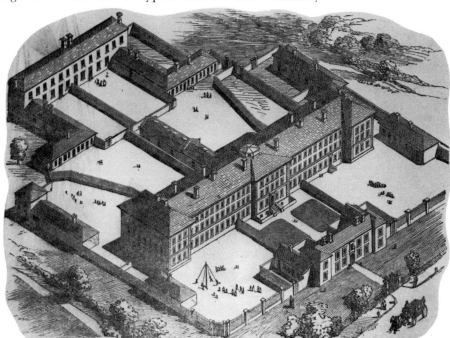

23 New workhouses were built in London. Under the New Poor Law only the destitute who had no possessions were admitted.

factory workers became almost a race apart, living in areas seldom visited by the middle classes.

During the 1820s and 1830s, middle-class volunteers formed societies to visit the poor in their own homes, to discover how real their needs were, to provide relief if it was thought necessary and to encourage the habits of prudence, industry and cleanliness, in which the poor were considered to be so sadly lacking. Many of these visitors were 'ladies', including single women, since charitable works were one of the few occupations regarded as 'suitable' for ladies, and which required little training. They were often deeply shocked by the abject poverty they discovered. Their visits were not always welcomed and they did little to promote friendly feelings between the classes, but they did lead to a deepening sense of concern in the middle classes and to the growth of other charitable societies. They also helped to establish what was later to become an important aspect of Victorian philanthropy, an emphasis on the careful study of the merits of each individual case before relief was granted.

The Ragged Schools
From the beginning of the century, educationalists had been pressing for the provision of some sort of state elementary education system for the poor — if only because it was considered inefficient to have an illiterate work force. But proposals by Samuel Whitbread and Lord Brougham for a national elementary education system paid for out of the rates had been rejected by Parliament.

Voluntary school societies were founded instead, the largest and most influential being the mainly Nonconformist British and Foreign Schools Society and the Anglican National Society. After 1833, the government began to subsidize the societies. Since many children were working ten or twelve hours a day, their attendance at schools was irregular, but Sunday schools and schools of

24 *Above left* John Pounds' school for homeless children.

25 *Above* The Brook Street Ragged and Industrial School, London. Ragged schools made a greater contribution to infant welfare than to education.

26 *Right* Lord Shaftesbury, champion of the ragged school movement and of many other good causes for helping the very poor.

industry gave them some rudimentary knowledge. However the destitute children of convicts, beggars and tramps who were usually dirty, verminous and ill-clothed were excluded and left to their own devices. Outcast children, for whom there was little or no employment, lived in the slums of every industrial town, children like Tom-all-alone and Joe the Crossing Sweeper portrayed in Dickens' novels. They roamed the streets, slept under arches or in open spaces and survived by begging and thieving.

In Portsmouth a crippled shoemaker called John Pounds distributed hot baked potatoes to the 'drifters', the homeless boys and girls, who slept out on the harbour quays. Gradually he befriended them and for 30 years he taught them to read and to write in a school which he founded over his shop — the first of the 'ragged schools'. Eventually his example was copied. In London, barns and stables were taken over by voluntary teachers who taught reading, mostly from the Bible, for this was a movement closely linked with Evangelical Christianity. The children were rough and undisciplined. They came to the schools for the food and clothing which were offered to them. Charles Dickens, who visited a ragged school in a district of London known as 'Jack Ketch's Warren', described how the children 'sang, fought, danced, robbed each other — seemed possessed of legions of devils'.

In 1844, a group of London teachers decided to form a Union of Ragged Schools. A newspaper advertisement asking for public support attracted the attention of Anthony Ashley Cooper, later Lord Shaftesbury, who had spent his life championing the cause of the poor. Lord Shaftesbury was to be an important link between philanthropy and government. He was directly involved in many charities, but his main work lay in Parliament as a social legislator. Ashley took up the cause of the ragged schools with enthusiasm and became president of the Union. Speaking in Parliament in 1848, he produced some striking statistics: of the children in 15 ragged schools, 162 had been in prison, 116 had run away from home because of ill-treatment, 253 lived by begging and 306 had lost one or both parents.

By 1861, there were 176 ragged schools throughout the country. They offered little education as such, except in Bible study, and their main contribution lay not in education but in social welfare, through the founding of clothing clubs, penny banks and fresh air holiday funds. Some organized emigration schemes, others placed the children in jobs as messengers or rag collectors. One offshoot of the ragged school movement was the Shoeblack Brigade, founded by John MacGregor, nicknamed 'Rob Roy', to serve the crowds at the Crystal Palace Exhibition in 1851, when thirty boys cleaned 101,000 pairs of shoes and earned £500 between them.

Above all, the ragged school movement was enormously important in influencing the care of underprivileged children, through men and women who taught and worked in its schools.

Dr Barnado and Mary Carpenter

Doctor Barnado came to London to qualify as a doctor before going out to China as a medical missionary. He became a superintendent of a ragged school and was so appalled by conditions in the slums that he decided to make the care of London's waifs and strays his life's work. He opened his own ragged school in a donkey stable in Stepney. One night a boy of ten named Jim Jarvis took him to see the other boys who, like himself, were sleeping rough on a nearby rooftop. In 1870, Dr Barnado founded a home for these destitute boys. He took as his slogan 'The Ever Open Door — no destitute child refused admission'. He introduced cottage-style homes where small groups of children lived together, with a school on the premises. Following Dr Barnado's example, many other children's homes were founded on similar lines, including those run by the National Children's Homes and the National Society for the Prevention of Cruelty to Children.

Mary Carpenter had also taught and worked in the ragged school movement. In the 1850s she began a campaign to change the criminal law relating to juvenile offenders. At that time children from the age of seven could be sent

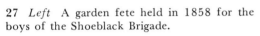

27 *Left* A garden fete held in 1858 for the boys of the Shoeblack Brigade.

28 Mary Carpenter whose ideas helped to bring about co-operation between private charity and the state in the care of deprived children.

to prison for theft. Mary Carpenter published a book with the formidable title: *Reformatory Schools for Children of the Perishing and Dangerous Classes and for Juvenile Delinquents,* in which she proposed that a series of residential institutions, managed by voluntary societies, but financed by both voluntary contributions and by state grants, should be set up as an alternative to prison for children found guilty of crimes. Her ideas influenced the framing of the Youthful Offenders Act of 1854, an important step forward, since it allowed for treasury contributions towards private reformatory schools to which the courts could send convicted children under the age of 16. Gradually, the state was beginning to widen the scope of its responsibilities for the welfare of deprived children.

The Evangelists

Strong religious feelings continued to play an important part in English philanthropy during the nineteenth century.

In the Anglican church, the religious revival known as the Evangelical Movement emphasized the need for social concern among Christians. A group of wealthy and influential young men, led by John Venn, rector of Clapham, worked for the improvement of the moral and physical conditions of the poor. Much of the credit for awakening public concern about conditions in the slums and for the campaign against slavery was due to them. They were active in campaigning for prison reform and for the setting up of ragged schools. They led the movement against cruel sports which resulted in the foundation of the Royal Society for the Prevention of Cruelty to Animals in 1824. Hannah More, William Wilberforce, Lord Shaftesbury and Dr Barnardo were all Evangelical Christians. William Wilberforce, who was a leader of the campaigns to end the slave trade and slavery, took an interest in 70 different charities and regularly gave away at least a quarter of his income.

Later in the century, in 1848, another group of young men formed the Christian Socialist Society to promote the peaceful reform of society through 'self help'. Led by F.D. Maurice, Charles Kingsley who wrote *The Water Babies,* and Thomas Hughes, the author of *Tom Brown's Schooldays,* they too stressed the need for Christians to care for the welfare of the poor. They worked to expand the co-operative movement, to establish temperance societies, life insurance and savings banks and to encourage slum clearance and adult education.

A great deal of highly emotional popular literature describing the hard life of the poor and the work of Christians in relieving it was written under Evangelical influence. *Jessica's First Prayer* described the life of destitute children in a large city; in *Ragged Homes and How to Mend Them,* Mrs Bayly described how lady visitors could help the poor to make the best of their lives. In *Haste to the Rescue*, Mrs Wightman described the horrors of drunkenness. All were widely read and helped to attract voluntary workers to charitable causes.

Magazines like the *Boys Own* and *Girls Own*, organizations like the Young

Men's Christian Association, 1844, and the Young Women's Christian Association, 1855, urged Christians to look after the less fortunate. The League of Ministering Children and the Sunbeam League were founded so that middle-class children could write and send toys to slum children who were ill.

Christian missions were set up to 'preserve and reform' the children of the poor, to help drunkards, prostitutes, criminals, soldiers and sailors, navvies, needlewomen, business girls and domestic servants. By the middle of the century Bible societies and lecture funds had proliferated, and large sums of money were also being subscribed to appeals for missions to the heathen overseas.

The Salvation Army

William Booth was a Nottingham pawnbroker who became a revivalist preacher. In 1865, with his wife Catherine, he launched the 'Christian Mission to the Heathen of our own country'. William Booth was a rousing speaker with a popular style. He soon renamed his mission the 'Salvation Army'; his followers were soldiers in the fight against misery, sin and want. His army marched through the streets wearing military style uniforms, following a brass band. 'General' Booth would call on his troops to 'Storm the forts of darkness!' to answering cries of 'Hallelujah!' Among his followers were 'Fiery Elijah, the Saved Sweep from Rugby' and 'A Milkman who has not watered his milk since he was saved'.

Salvationists were urged to 'sweep the gutters and seek the lowest'. They held 'midnight suppers' for vagrants and prostitutes. They opened homes for unmarried mothers and their children.

In 1890, William Booth published *In Darkest England and the Way Out*. 'A cabhorse has sufficient food, shelter and work', he declared, 'ought not a man to have the same?' He planned to set up farm colonies for the unemployed, depots for feeding the destitute and emigration schemes. Within a few months his supporters had raised £120,000.

Today the Salvation Army still runs homes for cripples and for the blind, children's homes, day nurseries and hostels for working men and women. Its mobile canteens work at the scenes of disasters; its 'midnight patrols' provide emergency accommodation for the homeless and for alcoholics. Its missing persons bureau has over 1,500 requests for help in finding lost relatives every year.

The Salvation Army and Josephine Butler between them created a voluntary 'moral welfare' service during the nineteenth century. Unmarried women with babies were often harshly treated by their families and by society. Josephine Butler championed both unmarried mothers and prostitutes. She visited them at work in the oakum sheds of the workhouses and in 1867 she bought a large house in Liverpool where, with the help of donations from local merchants, she founded an industrial home for 'fallen women', with an envelope factory and a laundry to provide work.

29 This Salvation Army Shelter, at Blackfriars in London, was nicknamed the 'Penny Sit-up'.

30 Josephine Butler (1828-1906) helped unmarried mothers and prostitutes at a time when they were often harshly treated by society.

One survey taken in 1861 estimated that there were at least 640 charitable institutions in London alone, nearly half of which had been started in the first half of the nineteenth century. Apart from the Christian missions there were many specialized agencies to help orphans, climbing boys, tramps, and lunatics. There were charities for the blind and the crippled, like the Shaftesbury Society for crippled children, which provided seaside and country holidays and 'cripples parlours', where the children made rugs and toys.

Forty specialized voluntary hospitals were founded in London between 1820-60, including eye and ear, heart, and children's hospitals. In Liverpool the District Nursing Association, founded by a local merchant named William Rathbone, advised by Florence Nightingale, grew into a national organization when Queen Victoria gave it the money subscribed by women for her diamond jubilee. Pension funds were set up for governesses and gentlewomen in distressed circumstances. Baths and wash-houses were built. Civic pride was shown in the building of fine town halls and universities financed, like the Great Exhibition of 1851, by money raised by public subscriptions.

Most of today's social services can trace their origins to voluntary societies founded in the nineteenth century. Funds were raised energetically. Voluntary hospitals held annual 'Hospital Saturdays', when supporters rattled collecting boxes in the streets. Ladies like Dickens's Mrs Pardiggle in *Bleak House* 'threw themselves into committees in the most impassioned manner and collected subscriptions with a vehemence quite extraordinary. . . shilling cards, half-crown cards, half-sovereign cards, penny cards. They wanted everything. They wanted wearing apparel, they wanted linen rags, they wanted money, they wanted coals, they wanted soup, they wanted interest, they wanted autographs, they wanted flannel. . .'

Charity became fashionable and received royal patronage. Prince Albert, for example, became president of The Metropolitan Association for Improving the Dwellings of the Industrial Classes. Charitable societies held splendid dinners and annual balls. They built impressive headquarters. Mrs Beeton included a model letter 'from a lady to another to aid a charity' in her *Complete Letter Writer.*

Those who practised it were sometimes gratified to find that charitable work could be a satisfying personal experience. One aristocratic lady who had been at the bedside of a dying man declared 'These little incidents made "slumming" a real pleasure. One gave so much happiness with so little trouble'.

Once again however, there was a growing concern over the proliferation of charities and a feeling that the poor were being encouraged to depend upon others, rather than upon their own thrift and self-reliance. It was claimed that many people were earning a living from begging. Well-known benefactors declared that they were being swamped by begging letters. There were examples of charitable gifts being pawned for gin! It was felt that more order and organization should be applied to charity.

31 Fashionably dressed ladies running a charity bazaar to raise money for the National Orphan Home.

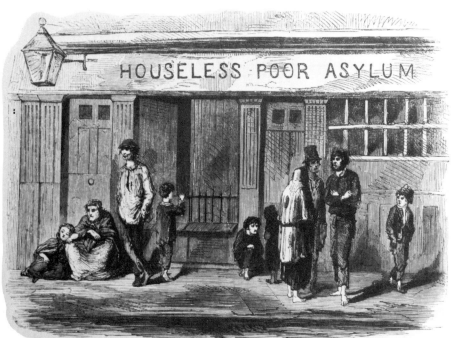

32 Hundreds of new charitable institutions were founded during the first half of the nineteenth century. Some people began to complain that the poor were being pampered.

5
Organizing Charitable Activity 1860-1900

The Endowed Trust

Since the sixteenth century, the most popular form of charitable foundation had been the endowed trust with an income derived from legacies or bequests. There were now many thousands of them. Some trusts were very rich and owned valuable property. Most individual bequests were very small, gifts made to almshouses, schools or churches, or as pensions or apprenticeships. The most numerous were the dole charities, small amounts of money, clothes and fuel, 'sea coles' or penny loaves, for distribution to the parish poor at certain times of the year. Some were completely out of date, like Week's Charity, founded in the fifteenth century 'to buy faggots with which to burn heretics'; others were eccentric, like Greene's Charity, endowed by a Mr Greene to supply old women with green waistcoats trimmed with green lace — to remember him by. Others could be shown to be harmful in their effect, like Jarvis's and Tancred's maliciously inspired charities, and the seventeenth-century Smith's Charity. Alderman Henry Smith, a London salter, had set up a series of trusts which included one of £1,000 for the 'poorest of his kindred'. His trustees invested the capital in property in Kensington and Chelsea. By mid-nineteenth century, this property had become extremely valuable, but the number of Smiths who all claimed to be descendants of Henry Smith had grown too. In one year, 23,000 people applied for financial help and received the sum of 4s 10d each!

The proceedings of the chancery courts which dealt with disputes over charitable trusts had become slow, cumbersome and costly and since the beginning of the nineteenth century law reformers had been demanding more public supervision over trusts and their administration.

The Charity Commission and the Endowed Schools

Lord Brougham was one of the leaders of the movement to reform charity law. He believed that the country's charitable endowments should be reorganized in order to contribute more to the common good, for example by providing the basis for an educational system for the poor. He led a series of parliamentary

MAYALL FECIT
JUNE 1ST, 1861.

33 *Above* Lord Brougham, Lord Chancellor of England, a law reformer whose investigations into charitable trusts led to the setting up of the Charity Commission in 1853.

34 *Opposite* During the 1860s poverty increased and many more beggars were to be seen in the streets.

investigations into educational charities, which later became a general survey
of the nation's charitable trusts, a process which took many years but which
led, in 1853, to the setting up of a permanent Charity Commission. Charity
Commissioners were appointed with legal powers to enquire into the administration of charities, to receive and audit their accounts, to examine trustees
on oath, to supervise the investment of charity funds and to adapt the objectives

of charities to altered circumstances where necessary (the power of *cy près*, see page 20).

By the 1880s, the Charity Commissioners had approved over 4,000 schemes for reorganization and some of the worst examples of outdated charities had been adapted to more useful aims.

Under the Endowed Schools Act, 1869, out-of-date charitable trusts which no longer fulfilled their founder's purpose could be converted to educational purposes, for example into scholarships at grammar and public schools. There was some criticism of this use of funds which had been left for the benefit of the poor, since scholarships for secondary education usually benefited the children of the middle classes. When the state finally took over secondary education provision in the twentieth century, however, the endowed schools remained, though increasingly dependent upon grants from public funds and under state supervision.

The City Parochial Foundation
The City of London was particularly well endowed with ancient charities. They included funds for sermons to celebrate the defeat of the Spanish Armada in 1588 and for ransoming Christian slaves held by the Turks, as well as many hundreds of endowments to buy clothes, bread and coals for the parish poor. By the late nineteenth century, some city parishes had become commercial centres and had virtually no 'eligible poor'. One old lady who lived almost alone in an area of the city taken over by offices and warehouses, liked to refer to herself as 'the poor of St Margaret's parish'.

By the Parochial Charities Act, the City of London endowments were extended to apply to the poor of the whole metropolitan area of London. Where the original purpose of the foundation no longer existed, funds could be used, through the City Parochial Foundation, for education, libraries, museums, open spaces or convalescent hospitals. London's polytechnics, the Old Vic theatre, the Whitechapel Art Gallery and many playing fields and recreation grounds have benefited, through the Foundation, from the City's endowments, and it continues to function today, helping to provide services to deal with many of London's problems, including alcoholism, drug addiction and mental illness.

Victorian Voluntary Societies
Most of the hundreds of charities which were founded in the first half of the nineteenth century were not 'endowed' charities, with incomes derived from legacies or bequests, but 'voluntary societies', which, like the eighteenth-century hospital foundations, were financed by donations given during the lifetime of the donor, or by annual subscription. Voluntary societies were not subject to any external control over the way they used their funds. Their organization could be altered at will. Between 1850 and 1900, voluntary societies became the most popular form of charity.

During the 1860s poverty increased. There was a succession of poor harvests and trade depressions and many hundreds of Londoners were made homeless by city 'improvements' and by the building of the railways. More beggars were to be seen on the streets and once again the blame was put on lax poor law administration and indiscriminate charity.

The Charity Organization Society:
Family Case Work and Hospital Almoners

Edward Denison, who worked with the poor in Stepney during the 1860s, was among those who were convinced that the answer to pauperism lay in more vigorous enforcement of the poor law and more careful co-ordination of charitable organizations. In 1869 he and C.S. Lock, who became secretary, founded the Charity Organization Society. Like the Poor Law Commissioners of 1834, they believed that poor relief should be reserved for the destitute only. They campaigned against indiscriminate charity: *A penny given and a child ruined,* was the title of one pamphlet issued by the Society. They urged that thorough inquiries should be made into each case of hardship before help was given, but in cases of real distress enough help was to be provided to put the family back on its feet again and to rehabilitate those who had been demoralized by poverty.

The Society recruited 500 voluntary visitors as well as paid officials and trained them carefully before sending them out to investigate cases of distress. Their policy of thorough investigation by fully trained visitors was to set the pattern for family casework in the state social services in the twentieth century.

Officials of the Society were convinced of the importance of investigating the home background of patients who were treated in hospital. In 1894, the Charity Organization Society and the administrators of the Royal Free Hospital together appointed the first hospital almoner, or medical social worker, to help the patient and his or her family with the social problems arising from illness. Until 1901, all almoners were recruited and trained by the C.O.S.

The Society published *The Reporter,* a weekly magazine advertising charitable appeals, and a handbook of charities, which is still published today as the *Annual Charities Register.* In its enquiry department, investigations were made into fraudulent charities and complaints about professional begging.

Voting Charities

The Charity Organization Society attacked the practice in many orphanages, almshouses and hospitals of admitting patients by election. Subscriptions and donations to a charity often gave the subscriber a number of votes, depending upon the size of the subscription, and the right to sponsor candidates for admission. A panel of eligible candidates was drawn up and an election took place.

In one year, 307 candidates were on the list for admission to the Royal Hospital for Incurables at Putney, but only 20 places were available. Charity elections were held at the London Tavern in Bishopsgate or at the Cannon Street Hotel. The walls were placarded with the names of candidates whose friends and relations canvassed for support for them from the electors. Election deals and bargains were arranged; sponsors would offer to exchange votes for 'three governesses' for one 'female orphan'. In many cases genuine candidates might wait years to be admitted to an institution. It was, in Florence Nightingale's words, 'The best method of electing the least eligible'.

In the 1870s, the Charity Organization Society launched a campaign against the voting charities and eventually brought the practice to an end. By the 1880s, the Society was growing out of touch with the realities of industrial poverty. It was often criticized for severity and unfeelingness. To C.S. Lock and his colleagues, poverty was avoidable through 'self help'. They saw nothing fundamentally wrong with the social and economic system and were sure that charity could cope with existing poverty without the need for state intervention. Therefore they opposed such schemes as the provision of free school dinners for needy children, on the grounds that they would cause families to become dependent upon charity. In 1910, C.S. Lock was to describe old age pensions as 'a huge charity started on the credit of the state', which he was sure would lead to demoralization as well as to vast expense.

During the twentieth century the outlook of the society's leaders gradually changed. In 1944 it was re-named the Family Welfare Association. Since then it has concentrated on family casework and on the training of social workers. Among many other activities it helps to run Citizens Advice Bureaux and administers trusts for minors until they come of age.

City Housing and Amenities

From the 1840s onwards, housing associations, like the Metropolitan Association for Improving the Dwellings of the Industrial Classes, were formed to build working-class homes and to let them at a modest rent. A small profit of about 5 per cent was aimed at, which was then used to build more homes. The 'buildings' were often depressing barrack-like structures of brick, surrounded by asphalt yards, but they were solidly constructed and were a great improvement on the tenements around them. They were usually fireproof, with each flat opening off a gallery; wash-houses and a bath were provided in the basement. Prince Albert, who was president of the Metropolitan Association, designed model homes for labouring classes which were erected in Hyde Park as part of the Great Exhibition of 1851. 350,000 visitors were said to have toured Albert Cottages, which each consisted of four flats on two floors, with a living room, three bedrooms, a scullery with a sink and a ventilated larder.

These works only touched the fringe of housing problems in industrial cities. The Peabody Trust, founded by an American philanthropist who had settled in London, had built 5,000 flats by the early twentieth century, but London's population had increased by 1¼ million in one generation. Rents for model dwellings were fairly high and could only be paid for by those in regular

35   Prince Albert's Model Cottages for the Labouring Classes, built for the Great Exhibition of 1851.

36   A view of Saltaire, once described as 'the largest and handsomest factory in the world'.

employment. The very poor remained in the slums until eventually housing for the poor was accepted as a public service.

Towards the end of the century, enlightened employers began to provide housing for their workers. For example, Titus Salt who owned a worsted factory in Bradford and who built a residential community called Saltaire for his 4,000 factory workers just outside the city. It contained a library, recreation hall, park, playing fields, schools and almshouses as well as homes.

Octavia Hill, a founder-member of the Charity Organization Society, was also concerned with the housing conditions of the poor. She bought up dilapidated houses, repaired them and let them to the roughest tenants, using women volunteers to collect the rents. Octavia Hill was a woman of wide interests and was also concerned with the threat to town and country caused by the huge growth of cities. In 1865, she helped to found the Commons Preservation Society, which campaigned and raised money to save Hampstead Heath, Wandsworth Common and Epping Forest from the developers. She decided that a nationwide organization to preserve the countryside was needed and in 1895 became a founder member of the National Trust.

Women and Charity

Elizabeth Fry was a busy Quaker with a family of 11 children who nevertheless found time for an immense amount of social work. Her chief interest was in prison reform, but she was also active in founding schools and shelters for the homeless. In 1818, she was summoned to give evidence to a House of Commons committee of inquiry into prison conditions, the first woman to advise the government on matters of public concern.

From then onwards, women were to play a large part in voluntary and charitable work. In the second half of the nineteenth century, the Women's Movement, which aimed at improving the status of women and opening the paid professions to them, encouraged women to stand for election as poor law guardians, school board officers and as part-time social workers, as well as to volunteer for charitable work.

Several women also made outstanding individual philanthropic contributions to society during the century. Among these was Angela Burdett-Coutts, who inherited a fortune from her banker great-grandfather and gave a large part of it away. She was an able business woman and managed her own charities, with advice from her close friend, Charles Dickens. She endowed churches and schools in the East End, supported ragged schools and many other charities for poor children. She built Columbia Market, Bethnal Green, to supply wholesale food at fair prices, and nearby four blocks of flats with a clock tower, to house 180 families. Costermongers were welcomed and stabling was provided for their donkeys. In 1871, Angela Burdett-Coutts was made a peer in recognition of her generosity and was the first woman to receive the freedom of the City of London.

37 Angela Burdett-Coutts.

Emma Cons turned a dilapidated music hall, called the Old Vic, into a centre
for working-class entertainment. She joined Octavia Hill in her campaign to
preserve open spaces and the countryside.

Mary Ward (Mrs Humphry Ward), a novelist born in Tasmania, founded a
settlement in central London in 1897 which became the first children's play
centre and non-residential school for crippled children.

Famous Victorian Philanthropists

The 1850s-70s marked the height of Victorian prosperity. Trade and industry were now showing substantial profits. From the 1870s onwards, wealthy industrialists made large donations to charity. Manufacturers, merchants and financiers founded universities, libraries, museums, art galleries and public parks and gave money to medical and scientific research.

Thomas Holloway for example had made a fortune out of selling patent medicines and Holloway's Pills were sold all over the world, but he had no children to whom to leave his fortune. As his wife was interested in higher education for women, he decided to found a women's university, Royal Holloway College, which was eventually to become a college of the University of London. The buildings were modelled on the French chateau of Chambord, and at first had only one lecture hall and no laboratories for the sciences. Once established, he allowed the college a fair amount of freedom in running its own affairs. Altogether Thomas Holloway gave away over a million pounds to charity during his lifetime.

Some wealthy industrialists were uneasy about the wealth they had accumulated through the efforts of working men. George Cadbury and his brother

38 The library of Holloway College in 1900.

Richard were Birmingham chocolate manufacturers who worked hard to build up the business they had inherited from their father. George Cadbury was a Quaker. He considered that using one's money for the common good was just as important as creating wealth. When their business was successful he and his brother decided to use it as an experiment in social welfare and a model for other industrialists to follow.

In the 1870s, the Cadbury brothers opened a new factory on the outskirts of Birmingham. Around it they built Bournville, a model village with parks and wide roads and gardens to each house. In 1901, the Bournville Village Trust was founded, to improve housing and town planning conditions generally. The Cadburys had demonstrated that commercial success could be used to improve the health and happiness of the workers who had helped to produce the employer's wealth.

George Cadbury contributed to many other charities. He bought a newspaper, the *Daily News*, and campaigned in it against sweated labour and in favour of the introduction of old age pensions.

Andrew Carnegie who made a fortune in Canada came from a Scottish Chartist family and never forgot what it had been like to be poor. He too saw himself as a trustee, holding surplus wealth for the benefit of his fellow men. 'He who dies rich dies disgraced' he once said. He founded hundreds of public libraries in the United Kingdom and established the Carnegie Endowment for International Peace, as well as a general purpose charitable foundation called the Carnegie Corporation.

Samuel Morley, a pious nonconformist and a patron of evangelicism and of chapel building, bequeathed many gifts to the community. He helped Emma Cons's attempts to found a working-class centre at the Old Vic, and founded Morley College for working men in South London.

The Bitter Cry of Outcast London and the University Settlements
By the 1880s, the income of London charities was greater than that of the governments of Sweden, Denmark or Portugal. Yet poverty persisted. The years 1873-96 were a period of high unemployment and trade depression, focusing attention again on the poverty caused by chronically low wages and underemployment.

In 1883 a penny pamphlet was published by the London Congregational Union. It began,

Whilst we have been building our churches and solacing ourselves with our religion and dreaming that the millenium was coming, the poor have been growing poorer and the wretched more miserable and the immoral more corrupt. The gulf has been daily widening which separates the lowest classes of the community from our churches and chapels, and from all decency and civilisation.

The pamphlet was called *The Bitter Cry of Outcast London, an Enquiry into the Conditions of the Abject Poor.*

From the 1880s onwards, the churches became more active in social work. The Methodist West London Mission, for example, later known as Kingsway Hall, was opened with an employment agency and legal advice centre for the poor.

At the same time, attempts were made to bring the upper classes more directly into contact with the workers. Canon Samuel Barnett, Vicar of St Jude's, a poor parish in Whitechapel, had previously taught undergraduates at Oxford. He founded a residential club in his parish, which he called Toynbee Hall, where young men down from Oxford could live while working at their jobs in London, using their leisure time to take part in the life of a slum neighbourhood. C.R. Atlee, who was Prime Minister from 1945 to 1951; R.H. Tawney, the historian; and William Beveridge, the social administrator, all lived for a time at Toynbee Hall as young men and acknowledged the great influence it had on their outlook and opinions. Many similar settlements followed, mostly associated with a university or school.

Charles Booth and Seebohm Rowntree

During the 1880s and 1890s, two men demonstrated the extent of poverty and hardship which still existed in society. They used their own resources to produce the first detailed and full documented social surveys. Charles Booth, a former Liverpool shipowner, began to work on a study which he called

39 A shelter for homeless men run by the London Congregational Union in the Ratcliffe Highway (1910). From the 1880s onwards the churches rapidly expanded their social work.

40 Charles Booth (1840-1916) spent 18 years on his social survey and pioneered new methods of social research. He considered that charity had not helped to solve the social problems which caused poverty.

Life and Labour of the People in London. Booth organized a house-to-house survey with the help of school attendance officers and he analysed the census returns of 1881-91. He produced information about the employment, hours of work and play, the size and state of homes, and the extent of unemployment of a million London families.

He found that one million people were living below a poverty line, which he set at £1 a week. He was convinced that most poverty was due either to inadequate wages, to unemployment, to old age or to sickness. In his opinion, the great outpourings of Victorian charity had done little to solve the problems of poverty. 'The people are no less poor. . . There are fewer paupers, but not any fewer who rely on charity'. He wanted the state to care for the aged on far more generous terms than the poor law had done and he proposed a state scheme of old age pensions.

Seebohm Rowntree published a study of poverty in York in 1901 which showed that Booth's findings applied outside London too. According to *Poverty: a study of town life* 28 per cent of the population of York were living below the minimum standard which Rowntree considered necessary for the maintenance of physical health. He described what he called the 'cycle of poverty', showing that in early childhood and in old age, most labourers could expect to endure poverty and hardship through no fault of their own.

These surveys made a lasting impression, not least upon future statesmen like Lloyd George and Winston Churchill. Mrs Pember Reeves summed up the concern felt by many people in a pamphlet called *Round About a Pound a*

Week, in which she contrasted the poverty of the poorest in Edwardian England with the luxury of the wealthy. 'If the poor were not improvident' she declared, 'they would hardly dare to live their lives at all'. During the 1890s, popular pressure grew for the extension of the public health service, for a system of universal free education and for reform of the Poor Law.

The Royal Commission on the Poor Law

In 1905, a Royal Commission was set up to examine the operation of the Poor Law. It produced two reports. Both agreed that the principle of the 1834 Poor Law, of deterring the poor from asking for help by the harshness of the terms, must be abandoned. They welcomed the planned introduction of old age pensions (by the Liberal Government in 1908) and called for an extension of free hospital treatment and more residential homes for destitute children. The Majority Report suggested that these reforms should be introduced through using existing voluntary organizations backed by local authority support. The Minority Report, which was the work of Beatrice Webb and her husband Sidney, wanted the complete break-up of the Poor Law and the extension of state social services to the sick, the aged, the unemployed and the mentally ill and to children. They wanted to develop a 'framework of prevention', to protect everyone, poor or not, against misfortune. The Webbs condemned the indiscriminate distribution of money, food and clothing to the poor. Through helping to relieve the symptoms, such charity was delaying social progress. Nevertheless, whilst they considered that major social tasks were beyond private charity, they felt that voluntary effort was still needed to aid and to supplement public authority provisions. 'We think that it should be a cardinal principle of public administration that the utmost use should, under proper conditions, be made of voluntary agencies and of the personal service of both men and women of good will'. They wanted a substantial measure of co-operation between voluntary and public bodies, but with voluntary effort playing the supporting role.

The Webbs were accurately foreseeing the mid-twentieth century welfare state.

41 Waiting for food parcels in Cheapside, about 1900. Social reformers like Sidney and Beatrice Webb believed that random charity of this kind delayed the introduction of state social services for the underprivileged.

6
Charity in the Welfare State

The Birth of the Welfare State

Between 1906 and 1914, a Liberal government passed legislation providing for old age pensions, labour exchanges, unemployment and sickness insurance, school health services and meals for schoolchildren, remand homes and juvenile courts for children in trouble. By 1914, the main responsibility for the welfare of the underprivileged had shifted from private charity to the state.

The 20 years between the two world wars were overshadowed by economic depression and unemployment. Hard times and high taxation affected charities badly. The great voluntary hospitals founded for the treatment of the sick poor in the eighteenth and nineteenth centuries were hit by rising costs. In spite of constant appeals for funds, flag days and poster publicity campaigns, many voluntary hospitals were on the verge of bankruptcy by 1939 and about 50 per cent of their income had to be provided by the government. After the

42 A 1911 Liberal Party election poster points out the benefits of their National Health Insurance scheme.

implementation of the 1929 Local Government Act, local authorities were expected to provide some of the hospital beds in their districts.

During these inter-war years, local authorities also extended their responsibilities to include slum clearance and housing for the working class and help for particularly disadvantaged groups within the community, the disabled and mothers with young children, for example.

In the 1930s, the problems of the depressed areas, those regions of northern England, Wales and Scotland where declining industries meant a high level of permanent unemployment, were so great that co-operation became essential between government agencies and charitable organizations in order to help those in need. The government appointed commissioners for the 'Special Areas' of high unemployment, who were authorized to give grants to voluntary organizations helping the unemployed. Many schemes were organized to encourage unemployed men to use their enforced leisure productively. The Society of Friends organized a scheme through which they could buy seeds and garden tools very cheaply. The Workers Educational Association and various adult education centres arranged special courses in working men's clubs. Centres similar to nineteenth century university settlements were established in areas of especially high unemployment, for example, Maes-yr-Laf, founded in the Rhondda Valley in South Wales and run by William and Emma Noble.

The Second World War put an end to unemployment at last and there was a general feeling that a return to such conditions after the war would be unthinkable.

The Beveridge Report, commissioned by the war-time coalition government, drew up plans for sweeping post-war changes in social security provisions, designed to establish a 'social minimum', below which no member of the community should be allowed to fall. The state was to provide a minimum income and to maintain a certain standard of health, housing and education for all.

In the years immediately following the Second World War, these plans were largely realized. The 1944 Education Act had already provided free secondary education; the National Health Service introduced comprehensive medical care in 1948; the 1946 National Insurance scheme provided pensions on retirement, widow's pensions, maternity grants and compensation for injury at work.

Since 1946 the government and local authorities have provided a range of social services which were once contributed and financed by voluntary effort. In the modern 'Welfare State', the old dependence on charity schools, voluntary hospitals, free clinics and private almshouses has been finally ended.

The State Welfare Services and the Voluntary Organizations
Many people expected that in the new welfare state, charities would no longer be needed. Charity was distrusted. It had become associated with the 'good deeds' of patronising Victorian ladies and gentlemen, typified by the wealthy

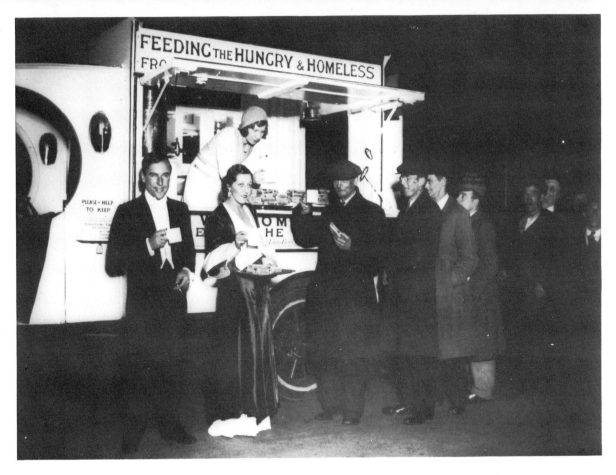

43 Amy Johnson, famous aviator, opens the 'Silver Lady's' night coffee stall for 'down and outs' in Trafalgar Square, 1930.

44 Classes for the unemployed were run at local authority evening institutes.

woman described in the 1905 Commission's report, who after hearing a sermon in church one Sunday morning went out into the streets distributing grapes and champagne to the poor. Indiscriminate charity during the nineteenth century was thought to have postponed much needed social reforms. Harold Laski, a leading socialist teacher during the 1940s, wrote that it was better to tackle social problems 'without the intervention of gracious ladies, or benevolent busybodies, or stockbrokers to whom a hospital is a hobby'.

45 *Left* This man did not want charity, he needed a job; but unemployment remained very high throughout the 1930s.

46 *Right* Sir William (later Lord) Beveridge arriving at the House of Commons for the debate on his Report in 1943. Beveridge had seen the effects of poverty at first hand when he lived at Toynbee Hall, the university settlement in the East End of London.

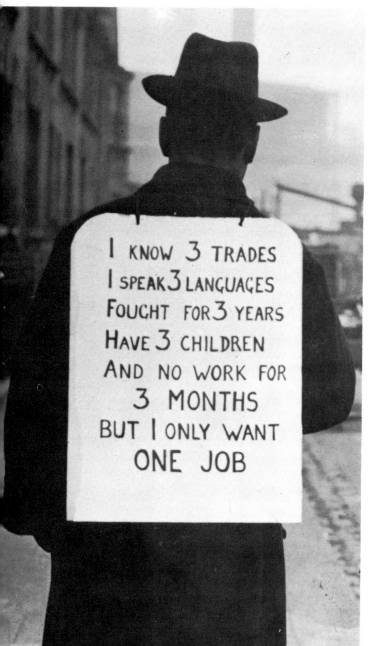

There were others, however, who like the Webbs, still regarded the voluntary spirit as essential to a democracy. William Beveridge, the author of the Beveridge Report, thought that the state should 'use where it can, without destroying their freedom and spirit, the voluntary agencies for social advance, born of social conscience and philanthropy'. Many millions of pounds were still controlled by charitable organizations and it was important therefore to define the role that these non-governmental or non-statutory organizations should play in a welfare state.

In 1950, the Nathan Committee was appointed by the government to examine the whole question, and in particular 'to recommend ways in which the goodwill of the past may be more free to serve the changing needs of the present'. Lord Nathan and his committee paid tribute to nineteenth century efforts to create a series of social services by private individuals, which they described as 'one of the most magnificent failures of our history'. They recognized the debt that the welfare state owed to the example of charities in the past; state action they declared was 'voluntary action crystallized and made universal'. Their report led eventually to the passing of a new Charities Act in 1960. It also led to much discussion and debate, during which many issues about the future role of voluntary action were aired. It was generally recognized and accepted that, once essential services are taken over by the state, voluntary effort is given a new freedom to seek out new needs and can play a valuable part in extending the frontiers of community care. Since that time, charities and voluntary organizations have established new roles for themselves in society.

One very important service that voluntary organizations can offer is help for people in finding their way through the often confusing mass of services provided for them by the state, the local authorities and charities. Just after the First World War, when central government had first begun to expand its welfare role, the National Council of Social Service was founded with both governmental and charitable support, to provide an information service and to give help and advice to voluntary organizations, individuals and government departments about finance, law, taxation and many other matters. The National Council of Social Service encourages citizens to take part in voluntary welfare work and tries to make sure that government, local authorities and charities co-operate. Before the war it helped to distribute government funds for the unemployed and to launch the Youth Hostels Association and the National Association of Boys' Clubs. It has set up the National Old People's Welfare Council, rural community councils and many other community organizations.

During the Second World War, when people were bewildered by the new and complicated controls and regulations made necessary by the war, the National Council of Social Service and the Family Welfare Association (the successor to the nineteenth-century Charity Organization Society) set up Citizens' Advice Bureaux, to deal with the many individual problems which arose from the war. Citizens' Advice Bureaux are run by trained volunteer workers. They still help thousands of people who come to them with a wide variety of problems over housing, social security benefits or insurance, family quarrels or education; they give legal advice and act as centres for consumer protection. As government has continued to become more complex and more centralized, this service has grown in importance.

After the Second World War, many voluntary services were taken over by the state. Others found themselves without a purpose any more, for example charities which had supplied medical appliances, such as artificial limbs, now provided by the National Health Service. Other voluntary organizations adapted their functions to work within the welfare state. Many local authorities which found themselves with additional responsibilities were glad to make use of existing charities, which were already experienced in dealing with certain problems, for example charities providing hostel accommodation for young people in care, and homes for the elderly. A patchwork of statutory services (provided by central and local government agencies) and voluntary services was formed, often co-operating closely. For example local authorities may rent out buildings at low rents to youth clubs or clubs for the elderly run by voluntary groups. They may provide paid staff or pay the salary of a youth leader in an otherwise voluntarily-run organization. They inspect and register voluntary homes in their areas.

The Care of the Elderly
Statutory and voluntary services work very closely together to provide care for old people. State pensions give the elderly a basic income; the national health service provides them with free medical care. Domestic help, laundry and meal services, clubs and recreational workshops are provided by local authorities either directly or through voluntary organizations. Social workers employed either by the local authority or by a voluntary organization work with the health services and with 'good neighbour' organizations like the Women's Royal Voluntary Service, which help to run lunch clubs, 'Meals on Wheels' schemes, social clubs for the elderly and many other services.

Both local authorities and voluntary organizations, such as the British Red Cross Society and the Central Council for the Disabled, offer advice and funds to provide home adaptations and aids which help elderly people to maintain their independence. Two voluntary organizations provide radios: Wireless for the Bedridden and Wireless for the Blind.

The National Health Service ambulance service is helped by the voluntary Hospital Car Service, the St John's Ambulance Brigade and the British Red Cross Society in taking elderly patients to and from their hospital appointments.

Age Concern, an independent charity, acts as a focal point for information and advice on all aspects of the care of the elderly. It recruits and trains volunteers for social work and has campaigned to involve local people, postmen and corner shopkeepers, for example, in keeping an eye on elderly people living alone. Its branches throughout Britain provide co-operation at local level between statutory services and voluntary societies concerned with the elderly.

The National Corporation for the Care of Old People, set up by the Nuffield Foundation, finances research into the welfare of old people and cooperates closely with Age Concern. The Pre-Retirement Association, set up as a charitable organization with support from industry, medical and voluntary bodies, studies the problems of adaptation to retirement. There are also many hundreds of local voluntary groups concerned with the welfare of the elderly, including church and youth groups, which help by looking after old people's gardens, decorating their homes, shopping, or just looking in for a chat.

Adapting to New Needs: The New Face of Barnado's

In the nineteenth century, Barnado's was a pioneering child care organization, providing children's homes at a time when there was no state provision. In the mid-twentieth century it has adapted itself to work within the welfare state. Like many other voluntary organizations, Barnado's now undertakes projects which government departments might not be able to justify financially. It concentrates on providing services in the more densely populated city areas, where welfare services are hard-pressed, working closely with local authorities to fill gaps and to tackle new problems. Since local authorities now run their own residential homes, Barnado's looks after emotionally disturbed children and the physically and mentally handicapped. It acts as an 'agent' for local authorities and accepts many children from the authority which then contributes to their upkeep.

Barnado's helps the families of mentally and physically handicapped children by providing holidays and periods of residential care. It provides day-care for small children so that mothers can go out to work, and to relieve mothers when they are ill, often after families in need have been referred to them by local authority health visitors, social workers or doctors. It runs play groups in the East End of London and play buses in Dublin and Newcastle.

Barnado's claims that as a voluntary society, it has the independence and flexibility to seek out previously unmet needs, which cannot always be provided for by the statutory services of the welfare state, though they may take

47 A member of the Women's Royal Voluntary Service (WRVS) takes a meal to an elderly woman living on her own.

them over in the future, when the value of these services has been demonstrated.

A Pioneering Role

In 1968, local authority social service departments were reorganized, following recommendations made by the Seebohm Committee. The Committee also looked at the role played by voluntary organizations in the social services. It foresaw them 'playing a major role in developing citizen participation, in revealing new needs and in exposing the shortcomings of services'. It emphasized the 'critical and pioneering' part that voluntary organizations should play in society. A certain level of ' "mutual criticism" might have to be accepted by both the voluntary and state services in order that the needs of the people benefiting from their services should best be served'.

As people have grown used to living in a welfare state they have begun to expect more from its services and to regard good health, for example, as a right. Parents of disabled children expect the state to do all it can for their children and when dissatisfied with the state's provisions they have formed their own organizations to campaign for better services, including advice and guidance from skilled professionals and the education of the public in the special needs of the group they represent.

The Spastics Society

In 1952, a group of parents met in a London hotel. They were worried and angry about what they considered to be the lack of facilities provided by the state and by local authorities for the education and treatment of spastic children. Spasticity is a disorder of movement and posture caused by damage to a small part of the brain controlling movement. It may cause speech, hearing and sight defects and sometimes mental handicap, though most spastics are very intelligent people who are well aware of their problems. Their condition can be much improved by early diagnosis and treatment.

The parents decided to form their own organization to press for more schools, residential homes and training schemes. They ran a successful campaign

48 Handicapped residents take exercise in the swimming pool at a Spastics Society's centre.

49 Learning the techniques of commercial horticulture at a National Society for Mentally Handicapped Children's rural training unit.

to raise funds and then found themselves involved in the provision and administration of the services they wanted.

Today the society runs residential schools for nearly 500 children, many in wheelchairs, homes for severely handicapped adults, family help units to care for children during family crises or holidays, work centres and sheltered workshops for those who are too handicapped for work outside. It has its own employment service and has set up a medical research unit at Guy's Hospital to work on the causes of spasticity.

Like so many similar organizations, the Spastics Society works very closely with statutory services. A residential home for severely handicapped men and women may be built by the society; the county council of the area in which it is situated will guarantee employment and the future running costs of the home will be met by the local authority.

Another association formed by and for the people who benefit from it is the National Society for Mentally Handicapped Children, founded by parents in 1947. It too tries through local societies to give help and encouragement to the handicapped and their families, and to support and complement the services provided by the state. Every year, Mental Handicap Week is sponsored by the Society, in co-operation with local hospitals. It focuses attention on the services provided for the children and tries to arouse further support from the public. As well as running its own residential and training centres and holiday and adventure courses for teenagers, it finances research into educational techniques for slow learners and training schemes for the care of the mentally handicapped. In its 'gateway' youth clubs, the mentally handicapped can share leisure pursuits, such as painting, football and dancing, with other young people of similar age.

Monitoring the Social Services: Shelter — a Pressure Group

During the 1950s, many people felt satisfied that the welfare state provisions had put an end to poverty. But a number of surveys made during the 1960s showed that real hardship still existed in certain sections of the community, among the old, the disabled, the unemployed and many single-parent families in particular.

Bad housing often contributes to family problems and Shelter was originally founded in 1966 in order to raise money for housing associations and agencies to help the homeless. However homelessness and other housing problems continued to increase and for this Shelter blamed the mismanagement of housing policies by successive governments. Gradually Shelter worked out a long-term housing policy of its own, lobbying members of Parliament and using the press and television to alert public opinion to the need it saw for a change in social policies and priorities. Its views are now widely respected and its members are sometimes asked to comment on new government housing proposals and circulars. From being a fund-raising charity, Shelter has evolved into a housing pressure group, which aims to persuade society to change its policies by influencing politicians and decision makers.

Many other societies have been formed to monitor governmental and other public services. For example, conservation groups like Friends of the Earth try to make people more aware of the risks of pollution and the need to conserve natural resources.

Participation in the Modern State

As government becomes more complex and centralized, there is a danger that people will feel that government departments and officials are remote and unsympathetic. Protest groups are formed when local amenities are threatened by new motorways or airports and local groups try increasingly to influence central planning decisions. Pressure groups formed to protect the underprivileged and inarticulate or to champion the users of the welfare services, can counter apathy and the alienation which may result from increased centralization. Consumers are no longer only those who pay money for a product or a service; they can be the recipients of the welfare services, or of charities themselves.

Long-established charities, such as those for the blind and the deaf, are also beginning to involve the handicapped themselves in policy-making and in the running of societies originally set up to help them. The National Federation for the Blind demands 'an equal say in our own affairs for the blind themselves', and is campaigning to get more blind people represented on local authority social service committees as well as on the Boards of Management of charities and other organizations for the blind. Participation of this kind can help the disabled and the disadvantaged to feel that they too have a part to play in society.

The Breakthrough Trust Deaf-Hearing Group was founded to draw the deaf and the hearing together through many joint activities, such as walks, jumble sales, dances, week-end courses and holidays. Voluntary societies and charities which are also self-help groups, or which aim to help other disadvantaged groups in society, can promote closer relationships and understanding and help people to forget their inhibitions and to enjoy each other's company.

Charities Which the State Will Never Take Over?

Some charities still provide services which the state is never likely to take over, for example animal welfare organizations like the Battersea Dogs' Home or the People's Dispensary for Sick Animals. There are also certain services for small minority groups in society which the public as a whole would be unlikely to support. By contrast, charities can still be found which continue to carry out a service which is essential to the community in general.

Perhaps the most striking of these is the Royal National Lifeboat Institution which was founded in 1824 and is still responsible for the fleet of lifeboats which operates around the coast of Britain. The lifeboatmen carry out many other services as well as rescuing the shipwrecked. They help holidaymakers cut off by the tide, they collect sick people from remote islands and take doctors out to ships. Although working closely with the Coast Guard Service and the Air-Sea Rescue Service of the Fleet Air Arm, the lifeboat service is not state-aided and does not seek to be. For a time during the nineteenth century, the service was supported by the Board of Trade, but there was so much resentment of the officials who supervised each station that voluntary contributions dropped sharply and so the Association decided to resume its unaided status. During two world wars, the government considered the voluntary system efficient enough to let it remain on an independent basis.

In 1975, the cost of running the lifeboat service was over £5.5 million. The money was raised from voluntary contributions, from collecting boxes, flag days, bequests and donations from business organizations.

The Lifeboat Institution claims that its system is efficient and effective. Local crews know local conditions best and only men of outstanding qualities volunteer for service. Local enthusiasm and pride ensure that each lifeboat station is run smoothly and that this is therefore a service which a charity can do as well as, or even better than, a government department. Several other countries in western Europe, including Holland, West Germany and Norway have also retained their voluntary lifeboat organizations.

Charities and voluntary organizations in the 1970s fulfil many real social needs. They provide an alternative social service which can monitor the statutory services. They often initiate new needs which central government or local authorities may then take over. They provide a service for minority groups which the government is unlikely to take over. Many people believe that every possible encouragement should be given to voluntary service and to the provision of private funds for charitable purposes. An active voluntary movement is often pointed to as one of the indications of a free and vigorous society. It can ensure that society maintains its standards of compassion and protection of the weak and disadvantaged. However, some charities are extremely rich and powerful bodies. Accordingly society maintains controls to prevent the possible misuse of their privileged position.

50 The Stornoway life-boat in action.

7
Charity Law and Administration, Twentieth Century Trusts, Overseas Voluntary Organizations

The 1960 Charities Act

Under the 1960 Act, a charity has to register with the Charity Commissioners in order to establish its charitable status, although universities, the British Museum and charities with very small incomes are exempt from registration.

The Charity Commissioners keep a copy of each governing instrument, the document which sets out the charity's objectives, and maintain a public Register of Charities. Registered charities have to keep accounts and make them available to the Commissioners if asked to do so. The Commissioners must see that charities use their resources effectively; they can investigate a charity and if necessary replace its trustees. They will advise trustees and order a charity to change its aims if they consider that the original purpose is no longer being sensibly fulfilled; the new cause must be as close as possible to the old one and to the spirit of the founder's intentions (an extension of the old principle of *cy près* ; see page 20).

The Commissioners encourage local authorities to review charities in their area, to bring their objectives and administration up to date and to co-operate with them where the services they offer overlap.

Charities are under the jurisdiction of the Chancery Division of the High Court. Their trustees may not sell or mortgage endowment lands without the consent of the Court. The Official Custodian for Charities can hold charity land, property and investment in trust for the charity.

The 1960 Act did not provide a modern legal definition of charity. To qualify for registration, a charity still has to conform to one of the charitable purposes defined in the preamble of the Elizabethan Statute of Charitable Uses, although that statute itself has been repealed. Broadly speaking an organization established for public rather than private benefit and not solely designed to make a profit will qualify as a charity in the legal sense if its objects fall into one or more of four categories, the relief of poverty, the advancement of religion, the promotion of education, or 'other purposes beneficial to the community'. The last category can include a wide range of charitable activities, from the repair of bridges, to the provision of sports facilities. Under the present law, charities may not engage in 'political activities'; they may not campaign to change the law or to try to influence government policy.

The Benefits of Charitable Status

In 1976, there were approximately 123,000 charities registered with the Charity Commission and about 2,500 are added to the register each year. The benefits of charitable status are mainly financial. They include exemption from paying income tax, capital gains tax and capital transfer tax, and registered charities qualify for rate relief on any building they occupy. Legacies and gifts to them may be permanent endowments, since only an organization which is 'charitable in law' can exist 'in perpetuity'. It has been estimated that the annual income of charities is well over £300 million and that the annual cost to the Exchequer of the financial privileges granted to charities is about £75 million a year. One recent estimate of the total value of charitable assets was £3,000 million.

Charities, Good Causes and Voluntary Organizations

In the modern legal sense the word charity only applies to organizations whose objectives enable the Charity Commissioners to give it charitable status. Many modern 'good causes' are not strictly charities in legal terms. However the term 'voluntary organization' can include all independent bodies, organizations, societies and agencies which are not run for profit, irrespective of their charitable status.

Voluntary organizations serving good causes vary widely. Some are organized nationally, with local branches; others are a federation at national level of many independent local bodies. All need 'grass root' groups to provide a service and a national organization to give information and to gather together the strands of local experience. A voluntary organization may be called a society, council, federation, campaign or standing conference. It will have an executive staff, some paid and others unpaid, honorary officials and committee members, voluntary workers and clients or consumers; sometimes these categories may overlap.

The National Council of Social Service recently compiled a list of the largest voluntary organizations in terms of financial assets and size of staff, which illustrates the wide range of voluntary organizations in Britain today. They include Oxfam, the Save the Children Fund, the British Red Cross, the National Association for Mental Health, the National Marriage Guidance Council, the National Association of Youth Clubs, the National Playing Fields Association, Barnado's, the Royal National Institute for the Blind, the Spastics Society, the National Council for Social Service.

Twentieth Century Trusts and Foundations

The charitable trust or foundation, administered by trustees on behalf of donors who gave special instructions about the way their bequests were to be used, has been a popular form of charity since the middle ages. In the twentieth century, a new type of charitable trust, a large general fund, not endowed for a specific purpose, and administered by trustees who often have a good deal of freedom, has been created.

Many of the largest modern foundations are government supported. The British Council, for example, founded by the Pilgrim Trust in 1934, was originally a voluntary organization supported mainly by business firms. Today it is an independent body, though largely financed from public funds, which tries to promote a wider knowledge of Britain and of the English language abroad and to develop closer cultural links with other countries. It maintains libraries and information services in many foreign capitals, makes grants to orchestras, museums and theatres and takes care of students in the United Kingdom from foreign and Commonwealth countries.

The Sports Council, set up to promote sport and recreation in Great Britain and to provide sports facilities, also receives an annual grant from the Department of the Environment.

The National Trust however, which protects 500,000 acres of countryside, much of it in the Lake District, Snowdonia and other National Parks, and many miles of unspoilt coast-line, is independent of the state and relies upon voluntary support for its working funds. It owns and opens to the public about 200 country houses, gardens, nature reserves and archaeological sites throughout the country.

Private Foundations

One of the largest private foundations is the Carnegie UK Trust, set up in 1913 by Andrew Carnegie with an endowment of 10 million dollars. Carnegie established public libraries in the United Kingdom and his trustees have tried to follow Carnegie's own charitable interests. When most libraries were taken over by public authorities, the trustees turned elsewhere, but the trust still sponsors rural library services and the problems of new towns — interests which they believe Carnegie himself would have pursued.

51 Story Hour at the British Council Library, Kandy, Ceylon.

The Wellcome Trust has an annual income of approximately £2 million, and was founded from the profits of the Burroughs-Wellcome pharmaceutical company. Burroughs and Wellcome were two American pharmaceutical salesmen who made a fortune selling medicines and pills in England. Almost all the money raised by the trust is used for medical research.

The Nuffield Foundation was created by William Morris, the motor car manufacturer who wanted to demonstrate the social value of great business enterprises. He had already given away £15 million to good causes, including the founding of Nuffield College, Oxford. His new foundation was intended for medical research, teacher training, educational scholarships and the care and comfort of the aged. Many of the projects sponsored by the Foundation today are in overseas countries.

The Livery Companies of the City of London have been active in charitable work since the middle ages, when city merchants entrusted them with the administration of their charitable trusts. There are still 87 Livery Companies functioning within the City of London. In 1969, nine of the largest administered charitable trusts which between them had an income totalling £1,550,000.

Private trusts help to direct a part of private wealth towards the public good. Since they do not have to raise money, private foundations can be flexible, they do not have to please customers, voters or subscribers in order to survive. Their supporters claim that they should therefore be much freer to experiment than government-sponsored bodies. Foundations can support independent surveys of government programmes and policies; they can take a fresh look at such institutions as the press, the professions, universities — and other charities. The more progressive foundations try to give support to small pioneering charities which identify with and deal with problems which can expect little popular support, such as drug addiction and alcoholism. The Rowntree Social Service Trust, for example, has foregone charitable status and the tax exemption which goes with it to help organizations such as Amnesty International and the National Council for Civil Liberties.

Private foundations often sponsor research which leads to new products. The work which led to the so-called Green Revolution, the development of new disease-resistent high yielding strains of wheat and rice which have helped to feed the world's growing population, was partly sponsored by the foundations. They have pioneered research into tropical diseases, and helped to establish the Palomar telescope.

Since foundations are privately owned, sometimes very wealthy, and usually enjoy tax benefits, they need to be responsibly controlled. Most of them review their policies every few years, to ensure that they are being used for maximum public benefit. About £130 million is channelled through private trusts and foundations each year and their critics would like to see more public control over the spending of these resources, for example by the government appointment of some foundation trustees.

Overseas Aid and Development

As more and more of Britain's own social needs were met by the state, it was natural that charitable people should turn more of their attention to countries overseas, where vast problems of hunger and disease continue to exist. Five major charities operate from Britain on overseas relief and development. These are Oxfam, War on Want, Christian Aid, The Save the Children Fund and Help the Aged.

Oxfam, originally the Oxford Committee for Famine Relief, was formed in 1942, by a group of people who were concerned about the suffering caused by blockades and shortages in war-time Europe. After 1945, hundreds of cases of hunger and homelessness were discovered in the devastated cities and the refugee camps of Europe, and the Oxford Committee launched many successful appeals for clothing, books and money to be sent to the refugees. The situation in Europe improved during the 1950s, but other problems emerged, for example the plight of Palestinian refugees and of homeless citizens during the Korean War. Oxfam gradually became a household word as it organized relief programmes to deal with both man-made and natural disasters. More than half of Oxfam's funds are spent on welfare projects, agricultural and technical training, hospital equipment and clinics. Its field directors and teams administer the schemes and work out how the money can best be used. There are Oxfam organizations in Canada, Belgium and the United States as well as in the United Kingdom, to raise money and support the schemes.

In emergencies people have to be fed and clothed, but most foreign aid agencies now also accept that they have a double responsibility; to help in famine situations, but at the same time, to provide 'aid in depth', to build up the economy of the country concerned and to help to train the people themselves for the production of food and the development of industry.

War on Want was formed in 1951 to press the British government to increase spending on overseas aid. Since then it has concentrated on providing long-term asistance. In Bihar, a famine-ridden region of India, it has sunk wells, encouraged cottage industries and provided the people with credit for buying cattle and seeds for crops. The Save the Children Fund, founded in 1919, provides medical clinics in Algeria and education for mentally handicapped children in Hong Kong; Christian Aid has training schemes for orphans in Korea; it teaches animal husbandry in Haiti and has built an agricultural training village in Tonga.

In 1966, the Voluntary Committee on Overseas Aid and Development was set up to encourage co-operation between overseas agencies, and to collect and exchange information. A United Kingdom Disasters Emergency Committee bringing together the British Red Cross, Christian Aid, the Save the Children Fund and War on Want, was formed to ensure immediate aid for national disasters and to administer appeals on behalf of all major overseas charities.

52 *Opposite* A young Turkish boy wearing a blanket provided by Oxfam after the earthquake in 1976.

53 An afforestation course in Guatemala. The Overseas Aid agencies train farmers in improved techniques of agriculture and conservation.

8
Charity Finances

Charity Income

Voluntary organizations obtain their income from many sources. They may receive grants from central or local government; for example, local authorities pay charities for the upkeep of children in the council's care who are taken into voluntary homes, though the payment may not always cover the full cost. They may receive payments directly from those to whom the service is offered, for example, Barnado's make a small daily charge for each child in its day care nurseries if the parents can afford it. They may receive a grant from a charitable trust or foundation. Some voluntary organizations can obtain money from membership fees, but most charity revenues still come, as they always have done, from donations. The Exchequer has made certain allowances which can increase the value of individual gifts to charity. For example by giving under a Deed of Covenant, part of the donor's before-tax income may be transferred to the charity and this income can then be exempted from taxation. Up to £50,000 may be left to charity free of capital transfer tax and an unlimited amount may be left to the National Trust, or to certain museums, art galleries and libraries.

Street and House-to-House Collections

One of the traditional ways of collecting money for charity is the street collection, often in the form of a flag day. According to a survey made in 1969,

54 The Mayor and Mayoress tour a poppy factory, where poppies are made for sale in aid of disabled ex-servicemen and women. The poppies are a reminder of the fields of Flanders, the battlefields of the 1914-18 war.

55 *Opposite* Hospital Saturday 1899. Since the 1890s street collections have been one of the most successful ways of raising money for charity.

Tuesdays and Saturdays are usually the best days for collecting money and Thursday is the worst! Perhaps the most well-known flag day is one held each year by the Earl Haig and British Legion 'Poppy Day' Fund.

House-to-house collections are subject to many rules. No collection for a charity may be made unless the organizers have obtained a licence from the police. Each collector must be over the age of 16 and must carry an identifying badge, and a policeman may ask anyone collecting for a charity to declare his identity and show his badge.

Disaster Funds and Broadcast Appeals

The public response to disaster appeals can still be overwhelming. During the Second World War, the Red Cross received a total of £54,324,408. In 1953, the Lord Mayor of London's Appeal for Victims of the East Coast Floods raised £5 million. In 1974, an emergency appeal on behalf of Ethiopian and African famine relief on radio and television and in the national press raised £1,400,000.

The BBC have been broadcasting charitable appeals since 1923. Up to 1975 they had raised a total of £19,000,000. Applications for television and radio appeals are considered by a special appeals department of the BBC and ITA and then by a Central Appeals Advisory Committee which chooses the appeals to be broadcast during the following months.

Trading Activities and Charity Pools

The sale of Christmas cards was one of the earliest and most successful charitable trading activities. In 1959 a group of about twenty charities, including Dr Barnado's and the British Heart Foundation, took over a number of empty shops for a few weeks before Christmas, in order to sell their cards. Now, through Help Cards, 29 different charities sell their cards in stationers and department stores, and the shopkeepers take one third of the profit. Other charities prefer to sell their cards directly to the public. The National Society for Mentally Handicapped Children sold £100,000 worth of Christmas cards through its trading company, Mencap Ltd, in 1975.

Separate trading companies set up by charities can covenant their profits to the charity. These profits are not taxed if they are solely for the purpose of the charity and the work involved is carried out mainly by those who benefit from it. Most charity shops are run by volunteers working on a rota system.

Oxfam has formed a separate wholesale and mail order company called Oxfam Activities Ltd. Its profits are covenanted back, tax-free, to Oxfam. Oxfam Activities runs a handicraft project called 'Bridge', which trades in rugs, belts, necklaces etc. bought directly from craftsmen in Third World countries. The goods are sold in Oxfam shops and part of the profit is then returned to the producers who belong to co-operatives and who undertake to use the money to develop the communities in which they live. The Bridge mail order catalogue tells the customer about the way of life of the producers as well as about the goods they produce.

Oxfam is planning to start handicraft co-operatives in Britain too, in old people's homes, among the mentally retarded, and in areas of high unemployment. It also raises funds by selling foreign stamps and, in some areas of Britain, by collecting and re-cycling waste.

In 1957, the owner of a small football pool promotion company in Bristol started a club called the Friends of the Spastics League, which paid twopence in every shilling subscribed by its members to the Spastics Society. Parents and friends of spastics became active local agents for the pool and soon the club had six million members. The organizers then founded a separate trust, called the Sembal Trust, from which other charities might benefit too. Other charity football pools have followed, raising more than £20 million between them and helping to provide special hospitals, schools and clinics for the handicapped.

Industry and Commerce

Many large firms, including Unilever, ICI and Shell, have special departments to handle charitable appeals. Shell, for example, reckons to give about £2 million to charity annually. Collections are often made by office staff or factory workers. The Save the Children Fund runs a Penny-a-Week appeal, approved by both the Confederation of British Industry and the Trade Union Congress, through which workers may arrange to have one penny or more deducted each week from their wage packets.

Local Events and Sponsoring

Charities still get much of their income as a result of the time and energy their supporters put into organizing local events, including jumble sales, treasure hunts, bring-and-buy sales, bazaars, donkey derbys, baby shows, pop concerts, student rags and countless others. The Variety Club of Great Britain has raised £8 million for sick and needy children since 1949. It organizes football matches, golf tournaments, film premières and many other functions.

56 A girl in a women's co-operative workshop makes a sita, a traditional food container. Oxfam sells them in its Charity Shops and returns part of the proceeds directly to the villages of Bangladesh.

57 The Bishop of Willesden starts a sponsored walk.

A sponsored event is a popular way of raising money, especially with children. Each person who takes part must find supporters who promise to contribute a given sum for each completed activity. There are endless types of sponsored events, such as walks, slims, silences, swims, digs and work-ins, even marathon snakes-and-ladders games! The Save the Children Fund suggests one useful sponsored event to its supporters, a sponsored 'clean-up' to remove rubbish from the countryside. The sponsors pay for each bag of rubbish collected.

Advertising

Publicity is a necessary part of fund raising. Charities are given special advertising rates by national newspapers, but even so, advertising is a heavy strain on a charity's resources and, to pay for itself, each advertisement must produce a strong response from the public.

Many people like to believe, perhaps as an excuse for their own lack of generosity, that charities are inefficient or mismanaged. Charities therefore often detail their expenditure in their publicity material or in advertisements in the press, showing the proportion of each pound donated which is spent on administration. Barnado's, for example, publishes a chart which shows how each £1 is obtained and spent, and the Save the Children Fund explains by means of diagrams where its money comes from and how it is used.

Advertising can also tell the public about the social problems with which the charity is concerned, making them care enough to involve themselves in those problems. Age Concern have run a poster campaign called 'The British Way of Life' to make people realize the need for care and concern for the aged; Barnado's publish a leaflet called 'Why Barnado's in the Welfare State?'

Why Do People Give?

The motives for giving to charity in the twentieth century are as varied as they have always been. Apart from generosity, people may give to create good will, out of pity, to gain power over others, to avoid embarrassment or suspicion of meanness. Sometimes good causes are supported for political reasons, or to preserve certain values and attitudes in which the donor himself believes, for social reasons or for fame.

Some charities use people's desire for fame and immortality in their fund-raising campaigns, for example, subscribers to the Royal National Lifeboat Institution have the privilege of naming a lifeboat. Many other benefactors prefer to remain anonymous. The University of London was given over £4 million for halls of residence for students on the understanding that no attempt was made to disclose the name of the donor.

58 Charities use a variety of advertising techniques in their campaigns. Age Concern tries to shock the public into caring more about the problems of the elderly.

PUNISHING THE OLD – A BRITISH WAY OF LIFE.

Condemned to loneliness.

AGE CONCERN
is action for the elderly.

Famous people are often asked to open fêtes or to give prizes at charity functions because their presence attracts visitors.

Advertising agencies hired by charities to help in their fund-raising campaigns have looked into the motives for giving and charity advertising reflects their findings. Since people give more readily to individuals rather than to anonymous appeals, many charities use case histories to 'personalize' their appeals. People are more easily moved by the thought of children in distress and many charities use the theme that the innocent usually suffer most in any tragedy.

Making people feel guilty may cause them to shut their minds to an appeal; a more successful approach may be to make them realize that their contribution will help. The National Association of Mentally Handicapped Children shows a cheerful child trying to do up his shoelace and the caption reads: 'With a little help from my friends'. The British Leprosy Association relies upon arousing feelings of pity. Oxfam and Christian Aid posters sometimes use shock tactics. A Christian Aid poster 'Ignore the Hungry and they'll go away' showed row upon row of gravestones.

Popular and Unpopular Causes

According to a survey carried out by *Which* magazine, the most popular causes for public generosity are medical research, children, handicapped adults, famine relief and animals. Causes which do not move the public are often those which deal with minority groups or interests, or which operate in controversial areas where the social need may be great, but the response from the public very small; in helping the victims of drug addiction and alcoholism or providing for the welfare of ex-prisoners, for example. This leads to inequalities in welfare and research raise many questions: should those in need have to rely on funds which may vary in amount depending upon the enthusiasm of their supporters or the success of the appeal campaign organizers? If resources are

59 Leslie Crowther, like many film, radio and television performers, gives up his spare time to charitable activities.

60 People are generous at Christmas time. Which charity will benefit from the money these carol-singers collect?

limited, who is to decide on the priority needs of society? They may not always be served by the most popular causes.

Lord Beveridge once proposed that there should be a voluntary service grants committee, endowed by the state as well as by foundations and by individuals, to give special attention to charities doing work of an unpopular nature. In Scotland, local 'common good' funds have been set up to raise money for all local charities or branches of charities, but with one or two exceptions, this idea has not been adopted in England and Wales.

Choosing a Charity to Contribute to

Christmas is the season when charities are most likely to seek out contributors. Carol singers call with their collecting boxes. Voluntary organizations post bundles of Christmas cards or send their collectors from door to door. How do you choose which charity to help? How worthy are different charities' aims? What services are most in need of money? How badly does a charity need your contribution and would it spend your money sensibly?

The *Charities Digest* published by the Family Welfare Association describes the activities of each charity and most charities will send publicity material, a simplified statement of account and an annual report if asked to do so. It is then possible to see how much money each charity raises from the public and elsewhere and its total income and expenditure. Since some voluntary organizations find it easier to attract money than others with less popular aims it is important to see what percentage of the total expenditure is spent on administration and how much of the voluntary income goes on fund-raising costs.

9
The Voluntary Worker in the Welfare State

Volunteers

Giving money to a good cause is only one way of helping it. Many thousands of people still give up their spare time to serve community needs and to help other people. Even in a welfare state, society depends for its proper functioning on unpaid workers such as school governors, justices of the peace or hospital committee members. Most voluntary organizations employ some full-time paid staff and increasingly use trained social workers, but honorary officers and committee members give their unpaid services generously and voluntary assistants help out with administrative work.

Volunteers run hospital shops and libraries, they visit the elderly and the disabled, they help to run clubs and tenant associations, take 'meals on wheels' to the elderly, act as foster parents or as prison visitors. Or they may work for the social services, in the education or consumer protection departments of local authorities. Some forms of voluntary service need specialized training: marriage guidance councillors and workers in Citizens' Advice Bureaux are carefully selected and trained before they start work.

Herbert Morrison, one of the architects of the post-war welfare services, praised '. . .these people who care about causes; the adherents, the supporters, the belongers; the chairmen, the treasurers, secretaries, committee workers; they have a special significance in our society'.

What is this special role of the voluntary worker in the welfare state? He can of course make scarce resources go further and release professional workers for the skilled jobs for which they were trained. But volunteers are not simply a source of cheap labour. Those who give up their own time are often the most compassionate people in society who have a real and urgent concern for the welfare of minorities and for difficult and unpopular causes. Probably their most important contribution lies in personal relationships with those in need, such as that offered by the voluntary associates who visit or write to prisoners and who give them help and advice during their first few days of freedom, 'a friendship without strings' which cannot easily be offered by the employees of statutory bodies.

In modern society, families are often scattered; people no longer live within easy reach of their parents or brothers and sisters and sometimes have no close friend or relation with whom to discuss their problems. The Samaritan movement was founded to help lonely and desperate people to find relief through talking on the telephone about their problems. Samaritan volunteers are trained to listen and to encourage a caller to talk. They man telephones in every large town and in some rural districts for 24 hours a day, every day of the year. Some Samaritan clients later become volunteers themselves, recognizing the tremendous value of the help they themselves received.

Mutual Help

Many voluntary organizations have been set up so that sufferers from a particular disability can try to help each other to overcome it; for example Alcoholics Anonymous, Gamblers Anonymous, Neurotics Anonymous.

The therapeutic value of helping others to those who feel lonely and unwanted, has always played a part in charitable motives. Age Concern are trying to involve the elderly in voluntary work in the social services, so that they feel useful and involved. The Spastics Society sponsors social clubs for the physically handicapped which are run by the handicapped themselves, although the able-bodied are welcomed too. The clubs encourage people to get out and about, through group holidays, sports meetings and conferences.

In 1972, the government, together with various trusts and foundations, provided funds to set up a Volunteer Centre, to encourage the use of volunteers in the health and social services and in voluntary organizations, giving official recognition to the value of voluntary service. In some hospitals a paid officer is responsible for the recruitment and use of volunteer workers within the hospital. Volunteer bureaux are run by local Councils of Social Service, with help from local authorities, to encourage the recruitment and training of volunteers in many towns. The Young Volunteer force, a government-sponsored organization, has set up centres to recruit young people for a variety of community services.

The Volunteer from Commerce and Industry

The Action Resource Centre was set up to encourage the secondment of professional and management staff from commerce and industry to help in voluntary organizations. Its management is drawn from industry, the government and voluntary services. Companies are asked to give their senior employees time off to serve as chairmen, legal advisers and consultants to voluntary organizations. Society as a whole gains when experienced people take a more active role in the community and the volunteers may gain fresh interests which will help them to use their working lives and their retirement rewardingly. Some firms also send their management trainees to work on community service projects; for example, under the Trident Scheme, executives work full-time for a year or more on projects involving young people.

The Young Volunteer

Voluntary service encourages an understanding of and participation in the economic structures and institutions of society, which is one of the important reasons for involving young people in voluntary work.

Community Service Volunteers was founded in 1962 by Alex Dickson. Volunteers from the age of 16 get board and lodging, travel expenses and a 'survival allowance', while they work on projects away from their homes. It is supported by many foundations, local authorities, firms and individuals. The volunteers are university graduates, police cadets, boys and girls from approved schools; some are themselves disabled or handicapped. They work in children's homes, night shelters, hostels for alcoholics, with Asian school-children who need to learn English, in subnormality hospitals or giving help to community relations officers. In Lancashire, approved school boys and prisoners, under the leadership of a seconded army sergeant, have taken over a derelict barge for renovation and to provide holiday homes for children and families in need. The Royal National Institute for the Blind sends young people

61 A young volunteer tells a story to children on a play bus in Ealing.

62 Community Service Volunteers put the last touches of paint to the renovated barge *Juno*.

as volunteers on CSV projects. CSV works closely with many other charities, for example with Task Force, a charity which works with pensioners to improve their conditions through the education and involvement of young people in the care of the elderly, and with MIND, the National Association for Mental Health.

Des Wilson, a former director of Shelter, the housing pressure group, has found that young people are not willing to plug gaps in the welfare services as a form of cheap labour. They want to know 'Why the gaps are there, and

63 Volunteers help on a National Society for Mentally Handicapped Children's adventure holiday in Cornwall.

whether they are being employed to hide them. . . they want to analyse community problems and devise their own role as prodders of the system'.

One of the functions of voluntary work is to give volunteers a chance to enjoy recreational or educational experience from the work. Young people work on many environmental schemes. For example, the Nature Conservation Corps which is part of the British Trust for Conservation Volunteers organizes work camps to carry out a wide variety of jobs, ranging from tree planting to the restoration of windmills and the preservation of Iron-Age fortifications. Volunteers may find themselves laying paths to reduce erosion on moorlands and sand dunes, digging out overgrown ponds, or clearing towpaths and canal banks.

International Voluntary Service

IVS was founded after the First World War by Pierre Ceresole, a Swiss pacifist. Its first United Kingdom work camp was held in South Wales, when volunteers worked with unemployed miners to turn a rubbish tip into a park and a swimming pool.

Today IVS runs international work camps where young people from many countries meet and get to know each other, and learn more about social and environmental problems. IVS volunteers work in hospitals for the mentally handicapped, they provide holidays for children from deprived homes, local

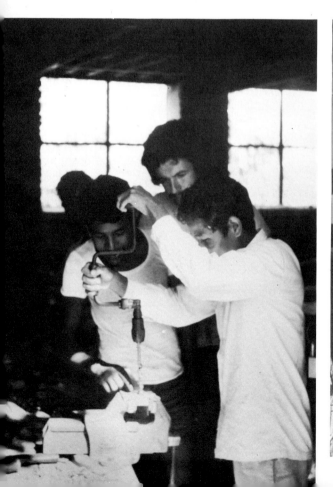

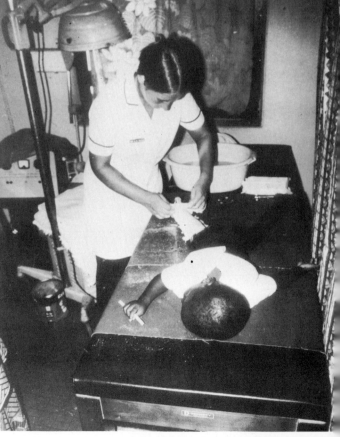

groups teach English to immigrants, and do decorating and gardening for old people. IVS sends skilled volunteers over the age of 21 abroad to work in agricultural, technical and medical projects in Africa and Asia, the cost being shared with the British Government.

IVS prefers to think of its schemes as giving 'community education', rather than as providing voluntary service. Volunteers often learn more than they give in return. Sometimes they feel that the work they do in mental hospitals or in the developing countries is a very small contribution to solving the problems they see. But the success of the projects depends on the way their experience is used later. Work camps are organized to allow for time to discuss the nature and causes of the problems which are being tackled by the volunteers. By understanding the frustrations of inner city life, or the reasons why the mentally handicapped are rejected by society, for example, they may help to bring about change.

Voluntary Service Overseas (VSO)

VSO is a charity which aims to provide a source of voluntary manpower to work in developing countries. Over 15,000 volunteers have gone abroad with VSO to more than 50 countries all over the world. When it was founded in 1958, its volunteers were young, unqualified people who were generally filling in a year between school and university. In the 1970s, the developing countries have more than enough of their own school leavers to fill the jobs the VSO cadets used to do. The volunteers who are needed most are those with a skill or qualification, teachers, doctors, nurses, agriculturalists, mechanics, plumbers, or engineers. Most are in their twenties, but there is no upper age limit. Volunteers generally go overseas for two years. They are provided with accommodation and a financial allowance, but no more than those of the nationals who do the same job. Their welfare is looked after by the British Council, which acts as VSO's overseas arm. VSO receives financial support from the government, but must contribute one quarter of the cost of recruitment, training and equipment of each volunteer.

VSO hopes to see the volunteers on each project replaced as soon as possible by local people, able and willing to do the job. To VSO the concept of voluntary service is something desirable in itself. In the future it aims to present its volunteers in less philanthropic terms, by emphasizing the benefits which the volunteers themselves receive. It hopes to introduce reciprocal schemes through which volunteers from the Third World come and work in Britain.

64 *Far left* A skilled engineer teaching village boys at a training centre run by Voluntary Service Overseas in Bangladesh.

65 *Left* A physiotherapist working as a volunteer in a state hospital in Nigeria. Volunteers can learn a great deal from their experience in developing countries.

10
Current Problems for Charities

Charities and Politics

Charitable trusts which take part in political action to try to change the law or to influence government policy are at present in danger of losing their charitable status and the financial privileges which go with it. Yet governments continue to become more involved with all aspects of human activity and many charitable organizations have found it almost impossible to pursue their aims without becoming politically involved. The National Council for Civil Liberties whose aims are openly political and the Disablement Income Group which campaigns for changes in the law, are not recognized as charities. The Child Poverty Action Group which has attacked government legislation, for example over the abolition of free school milk and increased charges for school dinners, has been warned by the Charity Commissioners that it could lose its charitable status.

At present the Lord's Day Observance Society and the public schools are charities; the United Nations Association is not. The Anti-Slavery Society and the Howard League for Penal Reform, which were both influential campaigning charities in the nineteenth century, would probably not be considered eligible for charitable status today, if they were not already charities of long standing.

Amnesty International is an independent voluntary organization which helps 'prisoners of conscience', people who are imprisoned because of their beliefs and who neither advocate nor use violence to obtain their ends. Local Amnesty branches 'adopt' political prisoners in groups of three, one from a Western nation, one from Eastern Europe and one from the Third World, and work for their release. But since it uses publicity and political pressure to secure their release, Amnesty cannot be recognized as a charity under present British law. (A separate fund which it has set up to give material help to prisoners and their families is recognized as a charity.)

Overseas aid and development charities also find it difficult not to become involved in the politics of the countries in which they work. Many relief workers believe that the poverty of the Third World can only be tackled through political change and new patterns of world trade. One group of young relief workers issued a statement in 1968 in which they declared that, while they recognized the value and humanity of the work done by overseas aid charities, '. . too often it is the equivalent of tossing sixpences into a beggar's cap; money given by those who have no intention of changing the system that produces beggars and no understanding that they are a part of it'. On the other hand there are critics of overseas aid and development work who object to large sums of money going abroad, where it may be used for the general economic benefit of countries overseas, rather than directly for the relief of poverty. They feel that voluntary aid sometimes makes government action less likely and that relief agencies may help the tax-payer in the receiving country rather than the poor.

Criticisms of Charity Law

Many proposals for changing the law of charities have been put forward. A Charity Law Reform Society has been formed. Its members include many of the voluntary organizations which are not at present legal charities for tax purposes. They have proposed a new category of charitable organization to be known as the Registered Voluntary Organisation, which would give an organization the financial advantages of registered charities under the present law but would leave it free to campaign on behalf of its cause. Another proposal is that all societies not formed for private gain should be entitled to Independent Voluntary Society status, but this would be giving public subsidies through tax exemption to societies and protest groups — even, for example, to black magic groups — with which the majority of people would not necessarily sympathize.

As a result of the widespread feeling that charity law is again due to be brought up to date in the mid-1970s, the Goodman Committee was set up by the National Council of Social Service to look at charitable law and practice and to suggest improvements which would benefit the work and development of voluntary organizations.

A parliamentary committee which also examined the role of charity and the work of the Charity Commissioners suggested that 'charity' should be redefined as 'the advancement of purposes beneficial to the community' for the purposes of registration and tax exemption. It called for the relaxation of the old principle of not allowing a charity to have political objectives. It recommended that only institutions benefiting the whole community should be given charitable status. It would like to see more power given to commissioners to investigate possible mismanagement of charitable trusts.

Inflation

Inflation has presented charities with one of their biggest problems in the 1970s, particularly those whose income is substantially fixed. In the year 1974-5, the administrative costs of charitable organizations were estimated to have risen by about 30 per cent. Unlike commercial companies, voluntary organizations have no customers to whom to pass on their costs and no end product to sell at a higher price. Cuts in government expenditure, which often accompany economic crises mean that less money is available for charities; companies and individuals are likely to give less. Many charities are threatened with closure as their incomes fall and their administrative costs — rent for office accommodation, salaries to employees, costs of food and fuel in hostels and residential homes — have continued to rise.

Charities which rely on grants from trusts and foundations find that they have problems too. Foundations are often closely linked with industry or commerce; for example, the Nuffield Trust receives much of its income from the British Leyland Car Company, the successor of Morris Motors. When business is not prospering, the foundation's income falls too.

Charities with overseas aid programmes are particularly badly hit. They have to find more money to keep up with inflation at home and also with the ever-increasing costs in developing countries too. Many have begun to concentrate on setting up projects using 'appropriate technologies', for example supporting schemes which use bullocks and manually driven pumps for irrigation schemes, rather than power pumps and which, at the same time, encourage farmers to help themselves.

Charities are worried about the future and forecast having to cut back future research and expansion programmes. Even dedicated voluntary workers find it difficult to continue to work without pay in times of continuing inflation.

Business Efficiency and Economy Measures
In times of economic pressure it is particularly important to make sure that resources are being spent on what is worthwhile.

Some charities have called in business efficiency experts, to examine and if necessary rationalize their organization. Some have moved out of central London, to find cheaper and more convenient office accommodation in the suburbs or the provinces.

The Charities Aid Fund has been set up to advise charities on their financial problems. Some charity administrators, however, are unhappy about too much emphasis being placed on financial efficiency, which may not always be completely in tune with the manner or spirit of an organization. Should charities invest their funds to obtain the highest financial return, in South African gold mines for example, or should they invest in problem areas, a housing project in a depressed region for example, which is also of social benefit, although the financial return will be lower?

In large organizations, the professional and executive staff may not always be in agreement with the voluntary staff. Professional administrators and skills may make an organization more efficient, but may not necessarily be close enough to the aims and ideals of the organization. Many of the executive staff enter charities from industry or commerce where the skills needed are not always the same as those needed in a non-profit making voluntary organization. Who is to decide the policy of the organization? Does it review its policy and outlook at frequent intervals? Should a charity pay the best rate for the best staff available, or keep salaries to the minimum? All these are problems which are brought to the fore when a charity needs to work to a very tight budget.

A Committee was set up under Lord Wolfenden by the Carnegie UK Trust and the Joseph Rowntree Memorial Trust to review the role and functions of voluntary organizations in the last quarter of the twentieth century, 'in the light of the increasing interdependence between state and voluntary effort and economic pressures'. Some of the committee's answers to the problems facing voluntary organizations in the mid'seventies are bound to have relevance to society as a whole, for charities have always been organizations through which society attempts to solve its problems.

Charity in the Future

The social services provided by central and local government are bound by law to carry out certain duties, such as the provision of education, financial support for the sick and unemployed and residential care for the old and infirm. As time passes, people expect continuously higher standards of care to be provided for the disadvantaged in society. Voluntary effort can fill the gaps between what the community demands and what the state can provide, until possibly the state or the local authority is able to take over the service, at the point which Lord Nathan has called 'the continuously moving frontier for philan-thropic action'.

Charities and voluntary societies therefore need to be very self-aware, to look carefully and continuously at their relations with central government and with other voluntary organizations. They need to review their objectives and to adapt them, if necessary, to changed circumstances. Now that Britain has entered the European Economic Community, for example, most charities look forward to co-operating with similar organizations in other European countries, exchanging information, and possibly setting up European societies, with international meetings and other activities.

Charities need to satisfy themselves continuously that there is still a relevant place for their particular kind of work. Shelter, for example, has already declared that 'we exist to put ourselves out of business'. Charities in the future may not regard themselves as permanent organizations, and sometimes the money they collect could be put to purposes which benefit the community more if spent in some other way.

Voluntary service has been described as a way in which we achieve things in our society which may never be done, or done so effectively, by other means. It is often a spontaneous reaction to new social needs and as such has immense value. In the future, as in the past, there will always be new situations in which charities can make a great contribution to the benefit of society.

66 *Overleaf* Teams of oxen raising water from a deep well in Bangalore, India. An economical method of irrigation and one which encourages farmers to help themselves rather than to rely on expensive imported equipment.

Further Reading

Bagley, J.J., *Life in Medieval England*, Batsford

Beveridge, W., *Voluntary Action*, Allen and Unwin

Bruce, M., *The Coming of the Welfare State*, Batsford

Clarke, R. and Davies, R., *A Chance to Share. Voluntary Service in Society*, PEP

Clay, R.M., *The Medieval Hospitals of England*, Cass

International Voluntary Service, *Annual List of Work Camp Projects*

Jones, M.G., *The Charity School Movement*, Cambridge University Press

Moorehead, C., *Helping. A Guide to Voluntary Work*, Macdonald

Morris, M., *Voluntary Work in the Welfare State*, Routledge Keegan Paul

National Council of Social Service, *Voluntary Social Services Directory and Handbook*

Nightingale, B., *Charities*, Allen Lane

Owens, D., *English Philanthropy*, Oxford University Press

Rowntree, S., *Poverty and Progress*, Longmans

Stephens, W.B., *Sources for English Local History*, Manchester University Press

Whitaker, B., *The Foundations. An Anatomy of Philanthropy and Society*, Eyre Methuen

Index

The numbers in **bold** type refer to the figure numbers of the illustrations